BBC MUSIC GUIDES

HUGO

BBC MUSIC GUIDES

Hugo Wolf Songs

MOSCO CARNER

BRITISH BROADCASTING CORPORATION

For

'HASELNÜSSCHEN'

Contents

Published by the
British Broadcasting Corporation
35 Marylebone High Street
London W1M 4AA

ISBN 0 563 17877 9

First published 1982

© Mosco Carner 1982

Filmset in Great Britain by
August Filmsetting, Warrington, Cheshire
Printed in England by Hollen Street Press, Slough, Bucks

Introduction: 'In the beginning was the Word . . .'

'On the whole I got the impression that I was *not* understood, that they busied themselves too much with *musical* matters and thereby forgot what is new and original in my musico-poetic conception. Continual chatter of musicians.' Thus wrote Wolf in a letter to Melanie Köchert about a meeting in October 1890 with some Munich musicians anxious to hear a selection from his Mörike and Goethe songs. These words conceal the essence of Wolf's philosophy as a song writer. We must not, Wolf implied, judge his songs as music *per se* ('they busied themselves too much with *musical* matters'), but solely in relation to the degree to which they succeed in recreating, in terms of voice and piano, the poem's words, mood and meaning. The music, in other words, makes no sense apart from the text. *Prima le parole e poi la musica* was Wolf's motto: the words are the alpha and omega of his creations and through the power of his 'musico-poetic' imagination, they fuse with the music into a wholly organic entity. The Wolfian song, it has been said, aspires to the condition of poetry. This is true, of course, also of Schubert and Schumann, but what distinguishes Wolf from them is his whole-hearted, self-effacing surrender to the poets of his choice, notably Mörike, Goethe and Eichendorff. Their verses are self-contained, tightly organised creations and *pari passu* a well-ordered disposition of verbal sonorities (the music of words), rhythms and inflexions. Wolf nearly always – the qualification 'nearly' refers to the Spanish and Italian volumes – submitted, as it were, body and soul to the poet's hegemony, which was an extraordinary achievement and something of a revolution in German song-writing of the nineteenth century. It defines Wolf's position in the history of the *Lied*. Significantly, in all the critical reviews that appeared after the publication of the Mörike songs, the word 'new' was prominent – 'Neuer Frühling', 'Neues Leben', 'Neue Lieder'. It was in this collection of fifty-three songs that Wolf's total, large-scale submission to the poet first took place, a fact that has been aptly, though not without a slight overtone of irony, called the 'Poetic Supremacy Act of 1888'. It was not merely a question of accompanying, illustrating and enhancing the words, but of assimilating and embodying them in music, which makes the typical Wolf song what it is.

Given this approach to song composition, one wonders what

5

Wolf would have thought, had he lived a normal span of life, of Schoenberg; Schoenberg who in 1912 declared that in many of his songs he went on composing – inspired by the sound of the first words in his text – without bothering in the least about the sequence of poetic events and images, and that he did not discover until several days later that he had never done greater justice to the poet than by following this method. Very likely, Wolf would have pronounced 'Anathema!' on the younger composer.

Before going any further, one point of intrinsic importance must be clarified. However great our admiration for Wolf for his scrupulously *literary* approach to song-writing, in the last analysis it is his *musical* invention, plus his technical craftsmanship, which must remain the ultimate criterion of his settings. Song is given its life-blood through music. To what extent this is true is best seen in Schubert. Admittedly, Schubert could be careless in the treatment of his words; he would often apply simple strophic form to verses containing stanzas of strongly contrasting sentiments so that the same melody has to do service for opposing moods; and he could be guilty of misunderstandings and misinterpretations of the poet's intention. Nonetheless, Schubert remains the greatest among the German song composers – partly for his prodigious output of some 600 songs, but largely for the well-nigh inexhaustible wealth, felicity and diversity of his musical invention. Schubert works almost entirely by instinct – Wolf impresses by the penetrating power of his musical intelligence. This has been described – admittedly with some exaggeration, yet not without a grain of truth in it – as the 'intellectualisation' of the German song, and examples of it are to be found in Wolf's settings of some philosophical and didactic verses of Goethe. The essential contrast between Schubert and Wolf may best be put as that established by Schiller in his great essay on naive and sentimental (reflective) poetry.

Wolf could learn nothing from Schubert's treatment of words, though a song like 'Der Doppelgänger', with its declamatory vocal line harnessed to an independent accompaniment, seems prophetic of what was to come in the younger composer's achievement. Wolf's true model in this and also other respects was Schumann – Schumann who, like him, possessed a refined literary cast of mind and paid, despite occasional lapses, far greater attention than Schubert to a correct declamation of the text. But it must be remembered that it was not really until Wagner that a scrupulous handling of words became a major principle of vocal composition, and it is probable that, apart from Wagner's chromatic harmony, Wolf imbibed a lesson from him for his own declamatory treatment. To return to Schumann, it was from the latter's great song cycles devoted to a single poet of outstanding quality[1] that Wolf took over the idea for his large volumes of Mörike, Eichendorff and Goethe songs. Yet, unlike Schumann's *Dichterliebe* and, in particular, *Frauen-Liebe und -Leben* (and also unlike Schubert's two Müller cycles), Wolf's are not cycles but collections that tell no evolving story but represent a loosely arranged series of character sketches, vignettes and mood-pictures, similar to a collection of paintings in a one-man exhibition. Wolf's aim was to display as many representative facets as possible of the poet's art, and he seems to have planned the scope of the volume in advance so that the whole seems greater than the sum of its parts. True, he composed the songs, haphazardly, in one order but published them in another, in which the placing of certain settings at the head or the end of a volume, or the pairing of particular settings, or the position allocated, *within* a volume, to a group of songs, takes on a symbolic significance. The Mörike and Goethe Songs and the *Italian Song Book* are conspicuous examples of this.

Probably taking a leaf out of Schumann's book, Wolf subtitles his various volumes in a characteristic and revealing manner: 'Gedichte von . . . für eine Singstimme und Klavier'. Two things are to be noted here. One is 'Poems' instead of 'Songs' in order to highlight the all-important role of the poet and his verses in the settings. The other is the conjunction 'and' in 'voice and piano', instead of 'voice with piano', which is as much as to say that the two are equal partners, each exercising its legitimate rights. Historically, Schubert was the first to raise the keyboard instrument from its largely subservient place in eighteenth-century songs to a crucial role in the projection of the emotional and physical situation of a poem. Schumann, a typically Romantic introvert, geared the piano part more closely to the inner, psychological element, as well as to the atmosphere of a lyric; at the same time, he made the interplay between voice and instrument more intimate. All this was taken over by Wolf and brought to its consummation. With him we reach the stage where the piano is not only collaborator but often becomes

[1] Rückert (Op. 37), Eichendorff (Op. 39), Chamisso (Op. 42) and Heine (Op. 48).

the senior partner of the voice ('Auf einer Wanderung', 'Prometheus', 'Geh, Geliebter, geh!'), so that one hesitates to speak here of 'accompaniment', a term that always seems to imply a secondary, subsidiary role.

The creative process in Wolf may be adumbrated in this manner: the basic mood of a poem ('Das verlassene Mägdlein', 'Anakreons Grab') or a striking verbal image ('Auf eine Christblume II', 'O wär' dein Haus durchsichtig'), or the metrical pattern of a line ('Jägerlied', 'Was soll der Zorn'), inspires the composer to a clear-cut and incisive characterising piano motive, and this forms the main brick with which the structure of the song is built up – either by varied repetition or by a developmental treatment of the thematic figure. At the same time, textual details are pointed up by suggestive melodic turns, harmonies and rhythms. With the mature Wolf, the musical substance of a song mostly resides in the piano part, and in presenting it he follows the formal principle of *absolute* music, while his *literary* concern is concentrated in the vocal line. Yet, strangely, Wolf shows a singular conservatism in his attitude towards instrumental phrase-structure. In the majority of his settings he adheres to a rigid 2 plus 2 or 4 plus 4 design, in which he goes at times so far as to add a completely superfluous pause bar at the end of a song, so as to make his regular structure fool-proof ('Begegnung'). An irregular phraseology is comparatively rare in Wolf. The regular phrasing assures Wolf of a firm, solid substructure. On this he sets a vocal line liberated from all purely musical constriction and going its own independent, word-inspired way, the line closely mirroring the inflexions, cadences and accents of the text, and lifting certain words of crucial importance to Wolf by a subtly calculated choice of intervals and pitches ('Zur Ruh, zur Ruh!', 'Um Mitternacht', 'Sonne der Schlummerlosen'). In essence, Wolf's method of superimposing a word-inspired vocal line on an autonomous piano part was the counterpart of Wagner's technique in his music-dramas, albeit on a different scale, and carried out with a heightened subtlety and refinement. This gain was not unexpected, given the intimate character of the *Lied*, which is to opera what chamber music is to orchestral music.

Wolf's formal designs are those established by Schubert – the A-B-A scheme, the simple and the varied strophic form, and the *durchkomponiert* or on-running through-composed conception. In his maturity we note a strong predilection for the varied strophic setting in combination with on-running treatment, while ripartite and simple strophic dispositions occur more frequently during his early period. But there are exceptions. 'Ganymed', for instance, is an A-B-A setting, and 'Morgentau' and 'Der Gärtner' – both in folksong vein – are strophic. Yet, even so ambitious a setting as 'Kennst du das Land', with its 'pathological' element, is cast into a but slightly varied strophic scheme, though its texture is very elaborate. And this brings us to Wolf's 'symphonic' settings – spaciously conceived and highly wrought songs in which the piano part is treated in a quasi-symphonic manner ('Im Frühling', 'Auf einer Wanderung', 'Auf eine Christblume I', 'Geh, Geliebter, geh!'). The qualification 'quasi-' is, I think, necessary, for Wolf scarcely ever resorts to thematic working-out of the Haydn–Beethoven order, the generally accepted paradigm of developmental technique, but prefers the (mostly varied) reiteration of motives and themes in changing harmonies, much in the manner of Mozart. Related to the 'symphonic' songs are Wolf's ostinato settings, in which a succinct and evocative melodic-harmonic figure persists, either literally or in slightly modified form, throughout the music. This is like an *idée fixe*, an obsession which occurs in settings of poems that convey thoughts and feelings of a haunting nature, as witness some of the sacred and secular songs in the Spanish volume.

Unlike Schubert, Schumann and Brahms, Wolf was not a born melodist, though in his folk-like settings ('Morgentau', 'Der Gärtner', 'Fussreise') he displays a most winning tunefulness. Where Wolf excels is as a harmonist of the late Romantic period, drawing on Wagner's rich harmonic resources for the suggestion of fine emotional shades and the play of tension and relaxation. Generally speaking, his diatonic writing stands for simplicity, directness, innocence and naivety; while his chromatic style is largely associated with complexity, many-layered feeling, arcane thought and the abnormal. The last is particularly true of the Harper and Mignon songs from Goethe's *Wilhelm Meister* and the Spanish settings referred to above. Wolf's chromaticism, particularly intense at moments of psychological stress in the text, tends to break up the framework of classical tonality and blur the sense of a definite key-centre. Even so calm a song as 'Phänomen' touches within sixteen bars virtually on every other key of the tonal spectrum in order to conjure up the image of a multicoloured rainbow. And, significantly, the harsh chromatic *appoggiature* of 'Seufzer' disconcerted Wagnerians even as late as the 1890s. Wolf was a master of the exploitation of chromatic harmony for psychological purposes, for illuminating a character's innermost thoughts and feelings, employing 'altered' chords, free suspensions and anticipations to pointed effect.

The chord of the augmented fifth is frequently used for the expression of intense emotions or, parodistically, of bathos – amusingly so in 'Bei einer Trauung'. And, making each of the three notes of such a chord, say, F-A-C sharp, the tonic of a new chord, Wolf arrives at his favourite succession of mediant keys as the symbol of growing intensity ('In dem Schatten meiner Locken', 'Die ihr schwebet') or increasing brightness of mood or elation ('In der Frühe', 'Ganymed'). (But his use of these *Terzrückungen* or mediant shifts is so frequent that they almost become a mannerism.) Wolf seems to have associated certain keys with certain moods and feelings: A major with the joy of spring, or A minor with a woman's distress and sorrow in love, the most notable example of which is perhaps 'Das verlassene Mägdlein'. D major was his key for contentment and elation ('Fussreise', 'Ganymed'), C sharp minor for night, sleep and death ('Um Mitternacht', 'Komm, o Tod', 'Sonne der Schlummerlosen') and so on. Extreme sharp and flat keys usually symbolise tension. All this must be taken into account when considering the delicate question of transposing a Wolf song.

A word or two about Wolf's piano writing. It is certainly not unpianistic, as it has often been described, but highly idiosyncratic, frequently intricate and difficult. Yet, with the exception of some quasi-orchestral passages, it always springs from the nature of the keyboard. In his early period, Wolf shows a predilection for hand crossings and often aims at a virtuoso style in the manner of Liszt or Chopin, a composer he much admired. Probably under the influence of Loewe and Liszt, Wolf wrote accompaniments that evoke the delicate tinkle of a musical box ('Nixe Binsefuss', 'Elfenlied', 'Zitronenfalter im April') and indeed, some settings give the impression that the brilliant piano part came first, and the vocal line was subsequently fitted round it ('Er ist's', 'Die Geister am Mummelsee', 'Lied vom Winde').

Wolf once remarked that the principal aim of his art was 'rigorous, bitter, inexorable truth – truth to the point of cruelty'. This realism, though rarely carried to these extremes, links Wolf with Mussorgsky

– Mussorgsky who two decades or so earlier subjected his songs to the dictates of the poem in an even more uncompromising, more daring fashion than did the Austrian. In contrast to the Russian's realism, Wolf's was of a psychological order, probing deeply into a character's psyche, often down to his unconscious springs. This illumination from within is particularly striking in some of the women portrayed in the *Italian Song Book*, who, through Wolf's music, are shown to have secret thoughts and sentiments undreamed of by the anonymous authors of these poems. This gift of Wolf's is matched by his power of drawing a bewildering range of different thumbnail sketches, particularly of lovers of every shade of passion, exultation and despair. No other song composer before or since has cast his net so wide and produced such a wealth of human vignettes as has Wolf. And only a musician of his artistic intellect was able to suggest dramatic irony by conveying contradictory emotions *simultaneously*, as the eighteen-year-old composer did for the first time in his Heine setting, 'Sie haben heut Abend Gesellschaft'. Where Wolf scores over the other great German song writers is in his highly developed sense of comedy – comedy of every kind: from the cabaret style of the Eichendorff setting, 'Die Kleine', to the drollery of 'Storchenbotschaft' to the parody of 'Bei einer Trauung' to the bogus monk's sanctimoniousness of 'Geselle, woll'n wir uns in Kutten hüllen' to the grotesque of 'Mein Liebster hat zu Tische'. Moreover, we know that Wolf had a most captivating way with young children and something of this comes out to entrancing effect in the childlike playfulness of 'Mausfallensprüchlein' and the charm of 'Elfenlied' and 'Epiphanias'.

For Wolf, every new poem was a fresh challenge to his inventive powers and in meeting it he displayed an astounding adaptability. In a Pickwickian sense, no two songs of his are alike. The protean nature of his genius allowed him to change his musical personality and, hence, his musical style with each of his great song cycles. Mörike, Eichendorff, Goethe and the authors of the Spanish and Italian volumes – Wolf may be said to respond to each in a different way, dependent on the poet's manner of utterance, the music of his words, the metric peculiarities of his verse and qualities of a more imponderable spiritual character. But there are constants in his *oeuvre* – recurring traits or fingerprints that help us to identify his musical vocabulary with certain poetic ideas. Eric Sams, in a highly perceptive study, has established over twenty such personal characteristics[1] – melodic, harmonic and rhythmic patterns which are Wolf's musical equivalents for concepts that form the stock-in-trade of the poetic imagination: love and despair, joy and bitterness, hope, loneliness and frustration, to which must be added musical stereotypes for the suggestion of other concepts such as sleep, night, mockery, companionship and the smallness of things.

In his early songs, notably those to verses by Heine and Lenau, Wolf wrote in a markedly subjective vein to which, one conjectures, personal experiences contributed their share. With growing maturity he came to adopt a more distancing – a more objective – attitude, banishing the intrusion of marked ego-related feelings and composing with the detachment of a keenly interested observer rather than one deeply involved in the emotional situation. The *locus classicus* of this objective presentation is to be found in such masterpieces as 'Das verlassene Mägdlein', 'Auf ein altes Bild' and 'Anakreons Grab'. The sentiments conveyed in the verses are not only recollected in tranquillity but sublimated to the highest possible degree. Wolf seems to disappear behind the words or, to put it differently, what the music has to say about the poem is said without the poem's identity being in the slightest affected by the composer's setting of it. The poet here becomes the musician. One feels that these songs have been composed for all time and once and for all. True, from time to time, Wolf relapses into his erstwhile subjective manner, but this now takes place on a higher level of artistic realisation. In such settings as 'Wo find ich Trost', 'Seufzer' and some of the sacred and secular songs of the *Spanish Song Book*, we seem to sense a profound personal involvement on the composer's part, particularly in songs about sin and redemption. Wolf was not a religious man (in fact he was something of an atheist) and hence his close identification with a sinner writhing in an almost pathological torment and agony cannot have sprung from a doctrinal belief in mortal sin. I venture to suggest that in those settings Wolf projected his own agonised feeling of guilt at his syphilitic infection or at his adulterous relationship with Melanie Köchert or both.

Wolf was a *Stauungskomponist*, that is, his creative impulses did not come to him (as they do with most great composers) in a steady, more or less continual stream, but were dammed up for months and even years on end; until the inner pressure grew so strong as to

[1] *The Songs of Hugo Wolf* (London, 1961), pp. 7–18.

burst the dam and release those impulses in a sudden tremendous flood. Wolf would then be in a state of trance and, with the sure-footedness of a somnambulist, write a song or two and sometimes even three in a day. There were three periods in Wolf's life of such intense creativity:

1878: Songs to words by Heine, Lenau, Rückert and Goethe
1888–1891: Songs to words by Mörike (53), Eichendorff (17), Goethe (51), Spanish Song Book (34) and Italian Song Book, Part I (22).
1895–1897: Der Corregidorf Italian Song Book. Part II (24), Michelangelo settings (3)

The last two periods fall into the final nine years of Wolf's composing life, and it has been calculated that in terms of actual creative work they scarcely amount to more than eighteen months – a unique case in the history of art; but this incredibly short span was long enough to place him in the front rank of German Lied composers.

It must be said, however, that Wolf demands, for a full appreciation of his art, an élite audience; this is so even in German-speaking countries where he enjoys less popularity than do Schubert, Schumann and Brahms. In other countries the listener must be conversant with the German language and be able to reflect on the content, imagery and prosody of the poems that provided the incentive for Wolf's great song collections. Reading the verses aloud, as Wolf frequently did himself, and comparing them with the way he set them to music, is a further help to an understanding of his particular approach. If Wolf was not a melodist in the strict sense of the word, his strength resides in the invention of succinct characterising piano motives and in a painfully sensitive treatment of the words. These are features more highly valued by the sophisticated lover of Lieder than by the average concert-goer, for whom beauty of melody and tunefulness are the prime criteria. It is, moreover, significant that, while each generation produces a fair number of excellent singers of Schubert, Schumann and Brahms, great Wolf interpreters are few and far between.

The Young Wolf

Wolf's earliest surviving songs date from 1875 when he was a boy of fifteen. Significantly, four among them were settings of Goethe verses. Indeed, already in his early period the young Wolf showed a large measure of literary discrimination in his choice of poets; besides such minor lights as Reinick, Hoffmann von Fallersleben, Zschokke and others, Goethe, Heine, Rückert, Lenau and Chamisso figure prominently among them. From the very beginning of his career song flowed from his pen with great facility and spontaneity, proving him a born lyrical miniaturist; while, with the exception of the D minor Quartet (1884), the symphonic poem, *Penthesilea* (1885), and the Italian Serenade (1887), his attempts in the purely instrumental field, which required thinking in terms of the larger forms, resulted in complete failures. Many of Wolf's youthful songs show insecure, tentative craftsmanship, rambling formal design and inept treatment of the text. Words are often repeated for the sake of achieving musical balance, and the simple or slightly varied strophic form is much in evidence. As an example of how unformed Wolf's immature style was at times, I quote a passage from Lenau's 'Frühlingsgrüsse' (1876), which almost recalls the vocal acrobatics of Bellini or Donizetti:

Ex.1

In December 1876 came Wolf's first Heine settings, of which 'Mädchen mit dem roten Mündchen' has the freshness and charm of a simple folksong. In 1878 he composed his first great spate of songs, when between January and October he set verses by (chiefly) Heine, Goethe, Rückert and Chamisso. In a letter written to a friend,[1] Wolf called that year 'my Lodi of songs, when I composed almost every

[1] This was probably an allusion to the resounding victory which Napoleon won over the Austrians at Lodi in May 1796.

day *one* good song and sometimes *two*'. This was also the year in which he began in Vienna his first passionate love affair, lasting for three years, his *innamorata* being the beautiful and high-spirited Vally Franck, his senior by four years. There is no doubt that this affair, with its ups and downs, acted as a most potent stimulus on his creative work. Heine (1797–1856) was the poet of unhappy love, and it was from Heine's *Buch der Lieder* that Wolf selected seven poems (there was originally to have been an eighth) to be gathered together under the title, *Liederstrauss*.[1] Schumann's *Dichterliehe* was in his mind when composing this set, but he deliberately chose verses not used by the Leipzig master; though he had the courage to challenge Schubert's haunting 'Ich stand in dunkeln Träumen'.

The *Liederstrauss* opens with 'Sie haben heut Abend Gesellschaft', which was the first example of Wolf's gift for dramatic irony: the lover's words of despairing sadness are set to music of a gay *Ländler* heard at his mistress's evening party. The probable model for it was Schumann's 'Das ist eine Flöten und Geigen'. 'Ich stand in dunkeln Träumen' cannot compare with the Schubert setting, but it is interesting for the Brahmsian influence seen in the contrapuntal texture, the piano theme appearing in augmentation in the vocal line. The third song, 'Das ist ein Brausen und Heulen', has storm-tossed octaves and driving syncopations in the accompaniment, which foreshadow his later masterpiece, 'Begegnung', in the Mörike volume. 'Mir träumte von einem Königskind' is a sad *siciliano* and a fine example of Wolf's declamation. Here the singer must characterise, by appropriate changes of tone colour, the dreamer and the object of his dream: a king's daughter who speaks to him from the grave. The exquisite piano part of 'Meine Liebchen wir sassen beisammem', recalling an arpeggio study by Chopin, suggests the sea and the plashing of oars. The song is in F sharp major, a key mostly associated in Wolf with a gay, rollicking mood, but here it serves to evoke a *triste* nocturnal atmosphere. The final setting, 'Es blasen die blauen Husaren', is the only gay piece of the set, and the first of Wolf's several vivacious military march songs. A lover has suspected his sweetheart of infidelity during the billeting of foreign soldiers in the village, but now that they have left he brings her, as a token of reconciliation, a bush of roses. The momentary blossoming out of the vocal line at 'Rosenstrauss'

[1] The seven Heine songs are, in addition to the Collected Works of Hugo Wolf, also available in the Peter Edition.

(Ex. 2) shows how Wolf throws into relief words charged with a special meaning or emotion:

Ex.2

The songs of the *Liederstrauss* show a considerable advance on Wolf's earlier manner, in that the basic mood of the poems is perfectly caught and verbal images set to incisive, sharply suggestive phrases. But the style is intrinsically Schumann filtered through the prism of Wolf's imagination.

In October 1878 came four more Heine settings, the text this time chosen from the poet's *Neue Gedichte*. Of these, the dark and tense 'Mit schwarzen Segeln' and the melancholy 'Spätherbstnebel' are the finest. Two years later (1880) Wolf added two more Heine settings, which are true gems and ought to be 'discovered' by recitalists. 'Wie des Mondes Abbild zittert' and 'Sterne mit den goldnen Füsschen' demonstrate already a characteristic aspect of the mature Wolf, namely the evocation of natural phenomena which, through the music, become animate, almost human personages. The first song at once recalls the later Keller setting, 'Wie glänzt der helle Mond' and the wonderful 'Der Mond hat eine schwere Klag' erhoben' from the *Italian Song Book*. The quiet, majestic movement of the moon across the sky and its oscillating reflection in the water are most imaginatively recaptured (Ex. 3a); while in the second song the twinkle of the stars and their gentle tread are conjured up with the utmost delicacy (Ex. 3b).

Wolf might have applied to these two songs what he said about another of his early settings – 'Man spürt schon das kleine Wölferl darin' ('You can already sense the little wolf cub in it'). He seems to have been far too strict and rigid when he excluded these and other Heine songs from his first publication of 1888. Admittedly, by then he had turned from a markedly subjective stance to a detached approach to *Lied* composition, but the two Heine settings of 1880

Ex.3

are singularly free from any *Ichbezogenheit* or ego-relatedness; and, what is more, they are very beautiful.

We turn back for a moment to that rich year of 1878 to glance at a single Goethe song which is quite unlike anything Wolf had written before. 'Gretchen vor dem Andachtsbild der Mater Dolorosa', from Part I of *Faust*, is the earliest example to show that painful, tortuous piano writing which was to become so characteristic of the Harper and Mignon settings and of some of the sacred and secular songs in the *Spanish Song Book*. It is also a highly interesting study of the emotional effect achieved by ubiquitous semitonal *appoggiature* in which one senses the influence of Wagner's *Tristan* (Ex. 4 overleaf).

Like Heine, Lenau (1802–50) was a writer who held Wolf's attention from his earliest composing days until 1881. The majority of Wolf's Lenau settings are in that sombre, self-tormenting and suicidal mood typical of this *poète maudit*, another syphilitic who ended his life in a mental asylum. Some of these songs certainly deserve a hearing, such as the intimate and tense 'Frage nicht', the grand 'Herbstentschluss' and the beautiful, dark-hued 'Herbst', all written in July 1879 when Wolf was deep into his unhappy affair with the fascinating Vally.

Robert Reinick (1805–52) was a minor poet of the Romantic school, but he has the merit that in his lighter verses he coaxes Wolf into displaying the more affable, genial side of his nature. Significantly, Wolf included two Reinick settings in his first publication

Ex.4

and resorted to this poet again as late as 1896. Of the five posthumous Reinick songs of 1883, the most successful are 'Frühlingsglocken', 'Nachtgruss' and 'Liebchen, wo bist du?', all of which contain numerous felicities. Thus, in the last-named setting, the lover wishes his sweetheart 'Goodnight!', his call being always echoed in the accompaniment, as in the example below, in which it is expanded and tonally altered. 'Liebchen, wo bist du?' has much to commend it for its amusing alternation of question (lover) and answer (mistress). It is a sparkling song, to be sung as fast as possible.

Ex.5

The First Published Collection

In autumn 1887 Friedrich Eckstein made Wolf the generous offer to have published at his own expense twelve of his songs written between 1877 and 1887, the choice of which he left to the composer. The collection, published in 1888, consists of two sets of six songs each, the first dedicated to Wolf's mother, the second to the memory of his late father. In view of the excellence of some of his Heine settings, it is legitimate to question Wolf's selection of songs, notably for the second set. With the exception of two or possibly three settings, the collection contains nothing that is really outstanding.

The first set opens with 'Morgentau' (1877), a setting of unremarkable verses which did, however, inspire the composer to music of pristine freshness and melodic beauty. In it Schubert (in the gently flowing accompaniment) and Schumann (in the shapely voice part) rub friendly shoulders, and the ending, with the singer's sustained D on 'still' and the piano recalling the opening, all in *pianissimo*, is sheer enchantment. The lyrics of the following song are by Friedrich Hebbel, best known as a playwright of great dramatic power. Of Wolf's three Hebbel settings (all 1878), two ('Das Kind am Brunnen' and the ballad 'Knabentod') are of little import, but 'Das Vöglein', with its bouncing vocal melody, the airy piano part, and its pictorialism – the bird's chirping and fluttering – though obvious, is appealing.

Rückert provided the poems for some of Schubert's and Mahler's finest settings, but his 'Die Spinnerin' (1878) found little response in Wolf. Yet the song is interesting in that it displays the young composer manipulating variation technique with much skill, and the keyboard writing demands an almost Lisztian bravura.[1] The two lullabies, 'Wiegenlied im Sommer' and 'Wiegenlied im Winter' (both 1882), after poems by Reinick, are engaging examples of Wolf's more affable aspect. The second song, richer in invention than the first, shows touches of a gentle humour.

[1] 'Die Spinnerin' happened to be one of a bunch of songs which Wolf showed Liszt at a meeting in April 1883 when the latter was much impressed by them.

The finest setting of the first set is 'Mausfallensprüchlein' (1882) and is a great favourite. In Mörike's verses, everything is on a minuscule scale – 'Kleine Gäste', 'Kleines Haus', 'Schwänzchen', 'Tänzchen'. Wolf's setting is a most delightful miniature, sounding as fresh and spontaneous today as it must have sounded a century ago. The sprightly, mercurial piano figures, the tiny runs, trills and grace notes are all in place – one feels there is not a note too many. It is a through-composed song, with an independent accompaniment into which the voice part is dovetailed with consummate skill. The playfully mischievous mood is typically and inimitably Wolfian.

The songs of the second set, composed later than those of the first, show – with one exception – a strange falling off of Wolf's inventive power, though every setting bears an individual stamp, notably in the harmonic language. The two Scheffel songs, 'Biterolf' (1886) and 'Wächterlied auf der Wartburg' (1887), written as a tribute to the recently deceased poet, begin promisingly but tail off in their latter half. Mörike's 'Der König bei der Krönung' (1886) is not one of his most inspired verses, nor is Wolf's one of his most inspired settings. But it is an effective piece, especially in its gradual preparation for the grandiose climax 'dass ich wie eine Sonne strahle dem Vaterland' ('that I may shine like a sun over the fatherland'). 'Beherzigung' and 'Wanderers Nachtlied' (both 1887) were Wolf's first published Goethe settings. In the first poem Goethe, rather sententiously, contrasts timidity, pusillanimity and hesitancy with courage, strength of will and dare-devilry, which accounts for the dichotomy of Wolf's setting. The first half sets out in G minor, much blurred by intense chromatics, while the second is predominantly diatonic in a clear G major. True, Wolf distils from Goethe's didactic verses the emotional substratum, but in the process he over-dramatises the verbal contrast. Far better suited to musical treatment is 'Wanderers Nachtlied', in which a disturbed soul prays for inner peace. It is torment rather than peace which Wolf projects in his markedly chromatic setting. Goethe's poem is couched in language of unaffected simplicity and directness, which Wolf rather ignores in his somewhat overwrought song, and which Schubert recaptures so wonderfully in *his* setting.

The finest among the six songs of the second set is 'Zur Ruh, zur Ruh!', to verses of Justinus Kerner, the poet who inspired some of Schumann's most sensitive settings. Wolf's music unfolds at a grave pace, conveying the weariness of the spirit in the stepwise chromatic descent of the piano treble in the first three bars. The great phrase of this song occurs in bars 13 to 16, in which the bold shape of the vocal melody symbolises the opposition of 'night' and 'light':

Ex.6

Nacht muss es sein, dass Licht___ mir wer___ de

Unfortunately, this song is sadly marred by Wolf's insensitive setting of the second half of the verses where, admittedly, the poet has nothing new to say. There was no room in these mystical verses for a crescendo to a shattering climax ending on a 6/4 chord, *fortissimo*, and with a top A flat in the voice part into the bargain. Wolf at twenty-three was still liable, for the sake of mere effect, to fall into the trap of utter conventionality.

Incidentally, 'Zur Ruh, zur Ruh!' and 'Morgentau' were the first Wolf songs heard in public, at a recital given by the celebrated contralto Rosa Papier-Paumgartner at Vienna's Bösendorfen Saal on 2 March 1888. The first verse of Kerner's poem was quoted at the end of Michael Haberlandt's oration at Wolf's funeral.

The Mörike Songs

Eduard Mörike (1804–75), a clergyman and teacher, led the un-eventful, placid life of a *Biedermeier*, which stood in so strong a con-trast to the life of his imagination. Influenced by Goethe on the one hand and by folk verse on the other, Mörike produced a body of poetry only belatedly (possibly through Wolf's settings) recognised as one of the treasures of German romantic literature. The conjunc-tion Mörike–Wolf seems to have been a case of elective affinity felt on the part of the composer, whose fifty-three settings (published in 1889) represent one of the high points of his creative career. Wolf's finest Mörike settings give the impression of having been written out of the very heart of lyricism, and this thanks to the peculiar quality of Mörike's verses, which are irradiated by a lambent glow and evergreen freshness of imagery. Add the poet's music of words and his formal perfection (largely springing from his pre-occupation with classical Greek and Roman poetry), and we come to understand why Wolf, himself a master of form, was so strongly attracted to Mörike. Wolf wished to give a panoramic view of Mörike's art – hence the wide range of his songs, encompassing, as they do, nature and the supernatural, realism and fairy-tale, the idyllic and the sinister, the humorous and the deeply serious, religion and mysticism.

Wolf's first Mörike setting of 1888 was the ballad-like 'Der Tambour'. But when it came to the publication of the songs, he placed 'Der Genesene an die Hoffnung' (twelfth in order of composition) at the head of the volume. It was a symbolic act, indicating that, like the convalescent of the poem, he had through Mörike been cured of his doubts about himself as a serious composer, and that his hope of achieving great and lasting things in his art had now become reality.

We begin with the love songs, the first three of which were all written in a single day (22 February). 'Der Knabe und das Immlein' is an entrancing piece, full of the fragrance of a spring morning. The dialogue between a youth and a little bee, to whom he entrusts a message for his sweetheart, might have come out of a fairy-tale. It is a song about young love, tenderly expressed in the voice part and with a lively accompaniment, punctuated by felicitous illustrative touches suggesting the buzz of the bee. The opening stanza is set to a somewhat tortuous theme (in G minor), perhaps too sad for a sultry day. Wolf turns this into an *ostinato* in the ensuing 'Ein Stündlein wohl vor Tag', which projects the heartache of the betrayed sweetheart who trusted the fine sentiments expressed by the youth of the previous song. The stereotyped refrain 'Ein Stündlein wohl vor Tag' lends the setting a measure of stylisation in the manner of a folk-song (as do the word repetitions in the wistful 'Agnes'). In each of the three stanzas the ostinato theme rises a semitone higher to characterise the girl's mounting pain, culminating in her outcry, 'O weh! . . . O still!', set to a fierce harmonic clash (voice: E; piano: F). The accompaniment in three and four parts suggests the string-quartet texture Wolf will use with frequency in the second half of the *Italian Song Book*. 'Jägerlied' is in a charming, lighthearted vein but is of lesser musical quality. It is Wolf's only song in genuine 5/4 time, not a compound of 3/4 and 2/4 or vice versa, and springs from the five stresses in Mörike's line:

Zíerlich íst des Vógels Trítt im Schnée[1]
(Daintily the bird doth tread the snow)

'Begegnung' is one of Mörike's most enchanting verses about the forbidden fruits of love: it has stormed during the night and there was also another kind of storm in the girl's room. Wolf recaptures this double meaning in a syncopated theme of intense agitation, which is the sole material in this song of sixty-six bars. E flat is its home-key and four more keys are touched on in its course. When the young lovers afterwards meet in the street in the morning, the notable restraint of the music seems to suggest the lovers' embarrassment as well as their quiet rapture. The very end of the postlude demonstrates Wolf's almost obsessional concern for regular phrasing, in that he closes with a rest bar in order to preserve his 2 plus 2 bar structure. (Bruckner showed the same obsession.) The poem of 'Das verlassene Mägdlein' had been used by some fifty composers before Wolf, including Schumann, but it is Wolf who set it for all time. The song is of the most remarkable simplicity and economy. Sadly despairing melodies in the voice part, with only a momentary flare-up in the middle to convey the deserted servant-girl's welling up of love, a funereal rhythm, cold sevenths and pathetic chords of the augmented fifths, and the whole bleak and depressing scene rises up before our mind. A comparison with Schumann's setting shows Wolf's more subtle psychological treatment by means of two interludes and a postlude (all missing in Schumann) in which the sad mood continues to reverberate.

'Nimmersatte Liebe' has great charm and delicacy. Only Wolf, one feels, could have set this Mörike poem about love's insatiable desire, with its rather explicit reference to female masochism (or male sadism?). The vocal line runs in a kind of stylised speech melody, evidently intended to allow the words to be distinctly heard, notably the climactic phrase 'Und anders war Herr Salomon, der Weise, nicht verliebt' ('Even for the wise King Solomon love was not different'), to be sung 'with humour'. The repeat of this phrase is set to a rollicking students' song to underline the debonair feeling of the text. 'Der Gärtner' and 'Zitronenfalter im April' are both delightful settings of a lighter calibre. The first is almost a folksong and deservedly popular for its winning freshness of con-

[1] Wolf was so taken by this unusual metre (a trochaic pentameter) that in a letter to a friend (Edmund Lang) he wrote out the whole of Mörike's poem and the first line of his song.

ception. But Wolf concentrates exclusively on the pictorial evocation of the princess riding gracefully by and ignores the humble gardener's adoration of the exalted girl. Schumann's setting pays due attention to the latter. The second song is all delicacy and grace but does not quite convey the inherent pathos of the verses. Wolf said about 'Erstes Liebeslied eines Mädchens' that the poem is 'mad and the music not less so'. The verses, with their phallic symbols (eel, snake), have invited some Freudian comment. The exceedingly brilliant accompaniment is a challenge to a pianist's prowess.

While the majority of Mörike's love poems are about the bliss and sorrow of imaginary characters, there is a small group of verses inspired by experiences of the poet's private life – the 'Peregrina' lyrics, 'An die Geliebte', 'Frage und Antwort' and 'Lebe wohl!' Peregrina was Maria Meyer, a mysterious and mentally unstable girl with whom Mörike was in love. She was obsessed of an incurable *Wanderlust* – hence the poetic pseudonym Mörike gave her. He eventually seems to have broken off what threatened to become a sexual affair. The five poems devoted to her are to be found in his autobiographical novel, *Maler Nolten*, of which Wolf set only two. 'Peregrina I' marks an early stage of the affair, while 'Peregrina II' shows Mörike haunted by a vision of the strange girl after he has cast her aside. The poet's language in these verses is of a feverish intensity, and this is mirrored in the composer's highly chromatic and overwrought style, notably in his second setting. The two songs, which are studies in the pathology of erotic love, are linked with each other in that the postlude of the first (Ex. 7) becomes the main idea of the second. As Sams has shown, Ex. 7 is typical of Wolf's love music and occurs in one guise or another throughout his career, and made its first appearance in the early 'Das Vöglein'. Its feature is the convergence in contrary motion of two strands of melody moving towards a unison:

Ex.7

Sehr ausdrucksvoll

Both songs are most deeply-felt music and yield their beauty only after repeated hearings. They are rarely heard in the recital room.

Mörike's 'An die Geliebte' and 'Lebe wohl!' commemorate his youthful passion for Luise Rau, the first expressing his initial happiness and the second his heartbreak at the ending of the relationship. Wolf's response to these fine lyrics is magnificent. In the first song we may feel that there are moments of over-dramatisation, but this does not at all detract from the general excellence of Wolf's conception. The declamatory flexibility of the vocal line, 'Von Tiefe zu Tiefen . . .' ('from depth to depths . . .') makes it appear as a composed rubato, and the setting of the closing line is one of supreme beauty: above high-lying, shimmering harmonies, the voice, beginning with 'Da lächeln alle Sterne' ('There all the stars are smiling'), gently arches up to the high G flat and then drifts down in a dying fall to the low E flat, when Wolf continues the vocal melody into the instrumental bass, *molto espressivo*. 'Lebe wohl!' is a moving farewell to the beloved, with the two opening words set to a variant of the 'love' motive (Ex. 7). The sadly falling semitones of the voice are echoed in the drooping tendency of all subsequent passages; a particularly beautiful demonstration of this is the great closing climax, 'und in nimmersatter Qual' ('and in endless pain'), when the voice drops down from top A flat first an octave and then a fifth to D below the stave.

To judge from their central positions in the volume (Nos 22 to 31), Mörike's religious verses must have had a special significance for Wolf. He was, as we said, not a believer but may have been attracted to some by their lambency and the beauty of their imagery; while to others, the theme of which is mortal sin and punishment, he may have been driven by his own feelings of guilt. The group opens with 'Seufzer', which is remarkable for its harmonic daring. The tonic chord of E minor does not appear until the very end of this song of thirty-one bars, which makes it a miniature counterpart to the Prelude of Wagner's *Tristan*; and there are chromatic double *appoggiature* lending the music a particularly dissonant character. No greater contrast can be imagined between the pain-racked expression of this song and the mysterious stillness and serenity of 'Auf ein altes Bild'. Wolf declared that, after finishing the song, he was still in the grip of the enchantment of its mood and, evidently referring to its opening line, 'In grüner Landschaft Sommerflor' ('In green, summerlike meadows'), said that there was still a green summery haze around him. The ancient (medieval?) painting seems to be suggested by the four-bar theme of the prelude, with its modal harmonies and organum-like progression in the treble. This theme occurs altogether six times and on its penultimate statement, at the words 'des Kreuzes *Stamm*' ('the cross's *stem*'), Wolf introduces a mild dissonance – a gentle hint at Christ's later suffering. Another superbly beautiful setting is 'In der Frühe'. Admittedly, there is nothing in the verses to indicate a specifically religious meaning, yet Wolf interpreted it in that sense. The first half of the song expresses the mental anguish and torment following a night without rest or sleep, which must have struck a familiar note in Wolf, who suffered from nerve-wracking sleeplessness himself. The rise from darkness to light is mirrored in the composer's favourite mediant key-shifts (the major mode of E – G – B flat – D) when the dull, tolling figure of the first half of the song returns as a distant, sweet chiming. With the morning all doubts and dejection have vanished. The poem of 'Schlafendes Jesuskind' was inspired by Mörike's meditation on a painting by Francesco Albani (1578–1660). Like the similarly inspired 'Auf ein altes Bild', it contains a passing allusion to Christ's fate at 'the wood of sorrow', conveyed by Wolf in an accumulation of dissonances in the piano part. Otherwise the setting is tenderness incarnate, with a prelude and postlude which are as a halo round the Christ-child's head. The theme of 'Neue Liebe' is the replacement of the imperfection of human relationships with God's perfect love. It is an uneven song – intimate and tender, and rhetorical and melodramatic. Of similar character is the spaciously conceived 'Wo find ich Trost?', with moments of a shattering impact at the words 'Hüter, ist die Nacht bald hin?' ('Watchman, is the night soon spent?') and their later repetition. The song is in strophic form and of progressive tonality, beginning in a sombre C minor and closing in a hopeful D major. The wide compass of the vocal part, from the high A flat to D below the stave, is indicative of its emotional tension. 'An den Schlaf', treating of the boundary between sleep and death, is virtually a monothematic setting and, like 'Seufzer', noteworthy for its *Tristan*esque harmony. By contrast, 'Zum neuen Jahre' is markedly diatonic and has the enchanting innocence of a children's nursery rhyme. The accompaniment, with its parallel thirds, evokes the sounds of a carillon welcoming in the New Year. The song foreshadows Wolf's Goethe setting, 'Sankt Nepomuks Vorabend'.

There is a handful of Mörike songs set to verses which convey a sentiment related to a religious mood, such as 'Der Genesene an die Hoffnung', a setting of grave nobility, and the delicate 'Denk es, o Seele!', which is about the intimation of mortality. The two songs 'Auf eine Christblume' are based on poems showing Mörike's mystic aspect. The drift of the verses is arcane and elusive – hence the various interpretations that have been put upon them, notably on the first. Only Wolf, with his extraordinary empathy with even Mörike's most esoteric visions, would have been able to follow the twisting thread of the poet's thoughts, reflecting his meaning in music of the most tender fragrance that is as the scent of the Christmas rose in 'Auf eine Christblume I'. Frank Walker, in his Wolf biography, has aptly described this finely crafted setting as 'an elegy, a nature picture, a religious meditation, a vision of elfland, and a hymn to beauty all in one'. The song is an excellent example of Wolf's ingenious combination of *durchkomponiert* with varied strophic form. 'Auf eine Christblume II', scarcely less mysterious of meaning, centres on a figure suggesting a butterfly hovering about the flower:

Ex.8   Sehr zart

This figure is constantly repeated as a piano ostinato, yet all feeling of monotony is banished by Wolf presenting Ex. 8 in continually changing harmonies and pitches. This kind of variation technique is very characteristic of Wolf's developmental method.

Wandering was a favourite subject of the German Romantics. Mostly, it is represented as the symbol of man's journey to the grave, as in Schubert's two Müller cycles and Mahler's *Lieder eines fahrenden Gesellen*. Wolf, however, seems to have taken the converse view, for, with the exception of the sad 'Heimweh', he chose two of Mörike's poems that give most eloquent expression to the exhilaration and blissful contentment the wanderer experiences. 'Fussreise', in varied strophic form, is one of the most appealing of Wolf's songs. Its vocal melody has the evergreen freshness and simplicity of a folksong; and it moves at the pace of a brisk march, with the wanderer's walking steps being tellingly caught in the lilting rhythm of the piano bass pervading the music from beginning to end. In the third stanza, in which the wanderer sings the praises of God the Creator, the voice part blossoms out into life-enhancing phrases that form the emotional and musical climax of the song. Yet 'Fussreise', infectious and ear-beguiling as it is, cannot be reckoned a great song. This epithet belongs without qualification to 'Auf einer Wanderung', which is indeed a supreme song by any standard. Mörike's verses take us into the very heart of a Romantic landscape – a friendly little town remote from the great world, young maidens, nightingales, a brook, and all bathed in the haze of a summer sunset. Wolf omits all pictorial touches and concentrates on the poet's delight and rapture at this idyll. The piano part is dominated by the gaily strolling 'Wanderer' figure (Ex. 9a) and, as we arrive at the visionary part of the verses, 'Ach wie liegt die Welt so licht' ('O world of bliss'), a little phrase is thrown up which is of magical beauty (Ex. 9b):

Ex.9

The free imitations in the left hand serve to heighten the significance of this 'yearning' figure (Wolf is said to have taken a fortnight, after the rest of the song, to complete this last section). At the poet's invocation of his Muse, we reach the luminous climax of the song, with Ex. 9b now repeated in a gloriously broadened (augmented) version. The postlude, which is matched by an equally extensive interlude, gradually ebbs away into nothingness. It is as if the wanderer cast a last glance at this Arcadia before vanishing into the darkness of the night. 'Auf einer Wanderung' is the example *par excellence* of Wolf's symphonic songs. Voice and piano go their own, independent ways, the vocal line joyfully lifting and dipping and the instrumental part unfolding in harmonic and (slight) rhythmic variations of the related Exx. 9a and b.[1]

[1] A small point but one worth mentioning: in the first stanza, Mörike

'Im Frühling' is another masterpiece conceived in Wolf's symphonic manner. The song is based on a motive which has a family likeness to the 'yearning' figure of 'Auf einer Wanderung' (Ex. 9b), and which in various guises pervades the entire setting. Here, as in the previous song, a feeling of a wide green expanse seems to be 'composed' into the music. The point towards which words and setting are working is the poet's answer to the question of his troubled heart: 'Was webst du für Erinnerung?' ('Tell me, heart, what memories are you weaving?') – 'Alte, unnennbare Tage!' ('Ineffable memories of the past!') is its reply. The vocal melody to which this last phrase is set appears to have fallen from Heaven – a truly divine phrase:

Ex.10

Yet Wolf had already anticipated it in the inner part of the piano in bars 3 and 4!

We now turn to Mörike's world of magic, dreams and the supernatural. 'Gesang Weylas' concerns the tutelary goddess of the imaginary island Orplid, invented by the poet. Wolf told Kauffmann that when composing it he visualised the goddess sitting on a reef in moonlight and accompanying her song on a harp. It is a noble, hymn-like setting, with a broad, incantatory voice part supported by solemn, hieratic harp chords, and was evidently modelled after Schubert's fine Goethe setting, 'Meeresstille'. Wolf's arrangement for harp, clarinet and horn enhances the magical atmosphere of the song.

The muted 'Um Mitternacht', which recalls another Schubert song, 'Nacht und Träume', has a similar accompaniment of gently

accentuates 'Und *eine* Stimme' ('and *one* voice'), to contrast it with 'Nachtigallenchor' ('chorus of nightingales'). Wolf seems to have overlooked this stress and, instead, underlines 'Stimme' on the strong beat of the bar, which makes little sense.

lulling, low-lying figures, above which floats a vocal line of exquisite shapeliness. Wolf closes each of the two verses of this strophic song with a bold, evocative phrase that seems to point forward to the Schoenberg of *Das Buch der hängenden Gärten*:

Ex.11

vom heu - te ge-we - se - nen Ta - ge.

The supernatural is represented in several of Wolf's Mörike settings. There is, on the one hand, 'Elfenlied', a delightfully playful setting, with an accompaniment as light as gossamer. And there is 'Nixe Binsefuss', which is as delicate as finely spun glass and in which, as in the later song, 'O wär' dein Haus' from the Italian volume, the melodic interest resides exclusively in the voice part; while the accompaniment evokes the image of the water-fairy in all her enchanting impishness. There is, on the other hand, the sinister 'Die Geister am Mummelsee' and the macabre 'Der Feurreiter'. Both are ballads probably written in tribute to Carl Loewe, for whom Wolf evinced great – indeed, uncritical – admiration. Loewe (1796–1869) was at his best in some of his ballads ('Erlkönig', 'Edward!') and songs in a lighter, more homely vein, but on the whole his melodic invention lacks real distinction. Whatever Wolf may have learned from him, such as, generally, a narrative style and, in particular, the 'musical box' effect in the accompaniment, he towered head and shoulders above the Halle composer. Even in such a setting as 'Die Geister am Mummelsee', which suffers from an over-elaboration of detail, Wolf proclaims his superiority in the way he gradually builds up the sinister menace of the opening and achieves an overwhelming climax at the end, when the narrator is dragged into the lake by the ghosts. There is a fine piece of illustrative music in the coruscating, Chopinesque piano cascades, suggesting the 'glowing water' of the text. Like 'Um Mitternacht', the ballad is in Wolf's 'night' or 'death' key of C sharp minor.

Mörike's highly dramatic ballad, 'Der Feurreiter', which shows the daemonic aspect of the supernatural, raised Wolf's imagination to white heat. There are at least five different themes, all very clear-cut and direct in their suggestion of the events in Mörike's legendary tale, and those illustrating the thronging crowd, the burning mill and the fire-rider storming away on his horse are used in the manner of leitmotifs. The setting is testimony not only to Wolf's inventive power at its most graphic, but also to his art of organising variegated musical material into an organic whole. Its tremendous rhythmic drive sweeps the listener off his feet. You may call it a symphonic poem that bursts the framework of a setting for solo voice and piano. Wolf must have felt this, for he later arranged the ballad for chorus and orchestra, which does more justice to its vividly dramatic character than the original version, and which was instrumental in spreading Wolf's name far beyond the confines of his native Austria.

From the *frisson* of 'Der Feuerreiter' to the resplendent comedy of 'Storchenbotschaft', one feels that only Wolf could have set the broad, *volkstümlich* humour of Mörike's ballad with such felicity and to such perfection. He invents for the shepherd a bagpipe tune which in several variations mirrors the evolving physical and emotional situations of the text. The *pièce de résistance* of the ballad comes in the final stanza: the *pair* of storks, after nodding their joyful affirmation of the shepherd's guess that he has become the father of *twins*, lustily fly away, to a hilarious waltz tune capped by a sustained top B flat in the voice part. It is an example of Wolf's *vis comica* at its most infectious. Another ballad, less droll than 'Storchenbotschaft' but full of good humour, is that of the homesick, sleepy drummer-boy in 'Der Tambour', conceived in the manner of a military march song. Its astonishing wealth of ideas is typical of the settings with which Wolf began a new period of prodigious creativity. (We recall that 'Der Tambour' was the first of the Mörike songs Wolf composed.) The quick succession of different moods ('importantly', 'lightly', 'pompously', 'perkily', 'tenderly') demands a singer of great interpretative flexibility. 'Der Tambour' is the pendant to Schumann's fine 'Die Soldatenbraut'.

Wolf's posthumous Eichendorff setting, 'Die Kleine' (1887), with its unequivocal sexual allusion, showed his talent for songs fit for the cabaret and the music-hall. The last five Mörike songs are characteristic examples of this. 'Zur Warnung' is a burlesque, ridiculing the notion that a hangover is best for inspiration. 'Auftrag' is in the style of a Viennese ditty and a suitable encore in a Wolf recital. Parody *par excellence* is 'Bei einer Trauung' – a mock-funeral march, punctuated by bathetic augmented chords, describes a society wedding in which little love is lost between bride and bridegroom. It must have been *Schadenfreude* or malicious joy that prompted Wolf to put 'Abschied' at the end of his Mörike volume: a pompous and self-important critic is kicked down the stairs – it is his 'farewell' – set to the tune of an exhilarating waltz *à la* Strauss. (Wolf seems to have forgotten that he had been a critic himself for three years.) The musical substance of these songs may be thin, but they make their point in a most diverting manner, and all are worked with the same meticulous craftsmanship as the products of his serious Muse.

The Eichendorff Songs

Joseph von Eichendorff (1788–1857) was an important lyrical poet, who excelled in the portrayal of a romantic landscape – ruins, dark forests, night and moonlight – through which echoes a mysterious, intense longing for another, ideal world. This is the Eichendorff of Schumann's Op. 39 (and of Hans Pfitzner's cantata, *Von deutscher Seele* (1928)). Wolf, in some of his early (posthumous) Eichendorff songs and several in his collection published in 1889, cultivated this vein not without success, as witness 'Die Nacht' (1880), 'Nachtzauber' (1887) and the Schumannesque 'Verschwiegene Liebe' (1888), an especially beautiful and *echt* romantic song, which contains a memorable phrase beginning with 'Gedanken sich wiegen' ('my thoughts are flying'). The acknowledged masterpiece among these romantic mood pictures is 'Das Ständchen', a song about the remembrance of things past. Memories of his youth and lost love are aroused in an old man who overhears a young student serenading his sweetheart – just so did he serenade his mistress of long ago. The voice part is solely concerned with the old man's soliloquy, phrase after wistful phrase following one another in complete freedom and independence of the accompaniment. The tenuous right-hand melody of it seems to suggest the student's serenade, with the evocation of a lute in the bass ostinato. The extreme transparency of texture is a special feature here. Only a composer of Wolf's musical intelligence would have been able to evoke, in a song of such simplicity, both past and present *simultaneously*. (The earlier Eichendorff setting, 'Rückkehr' (1883), may be cited as foreshadowing Wolf's achievement.)

Wolf, however, came to recognise that there was another aspect of Eichendorff, completely neglected by Schumann – his bluff, realistic humour, to which he directed his main attention. (But it must be averred that the public at large prefers his settings of the romantic Eichendorff.) Wolf's 'anti-romantic', objective Eichendorff settings present a wide variety of character sketches, in which soldiers, sailors, wayfarers, musicians, gypsies and braggarts jostle each other. 'Der Schreckenberger' and 'Der Glücksritter' (both 1888 and composed within three days of each other) are the songs of an engaging swashbuckler and are marked by rhythmic brilliance and great panache. They form a pair, which the composer underlines by quoting the pompous processional theme at the end of the first setting in the proudly strutting postlude of the second. Note the ingenious treatment of the march in the latter (in varied strophic form); and the setting of the final phrase, 'Alles zieht den Hut' ('everybody doffs his hat'), is inimitably Wolfian. Of the two soldier songs, 'Soldat I' (1887) is the more successful, Wolf enhancing its musical appeal by twice repeating the last line of the third and fourth stanzas (not in Eichendorff!). 'Die Zigeunerin' (1887), with its alluring melismatic triplet on 'la, la' and the 'Scotch snap' of the accompaniment, borrows from Hungarian gypsy music; it requires a mezzo-soprano capable of great virtuosity. Rumbustiousness is the key-note of 'Seemanns Abschied', which contains amusing pictorial touches, such as the snap of sharks and the scream of seagulls. The song opens with what was for its time a most strange harmony:

Ex.12

Bruckner is said to have been nonplussed by it when Wolf showed him the song. It is, of course, the whole-tone scale on B telescoped into a chord.

'Der Musikant' and 'Der Scholar' (both 1888) were written on the same day and have the same simplicity of style combined with pointedness and charm of invention. The first could almost be a folk-song, were it not for the lute arpeggios in the accompaniment and the unexpected modulation to a remote key, when the wandering minstrel expresses uncertainty as to where he will rest at night. 'Der Scholar' is a perfect, slightly caricaturing, portrait of a pedantic but amiable academic. Note the 'learned' counterpoint in the piano bass, with its alternating articulation staccato and non-staccato to suggest the young man's opposing moods. 'Liebesglück' (1888) is rhythmically exuberant and vigorous, but Wolf seems to have read too much into Eichendorff's innocent verses and overburdens the song with a self-important piano part.

As we have seen from the dates of these songs, Wolf included in his Eichendorff collection settings composed before the great year 1888, a few even dating back to as early as 1880 when he was twenty, and which were thrown in as a kind of makeweight. To these belong 'Erwartung' (1880), which is a highly alluring song in Brahmsian (!) style, with a teasing cross-rhythm between the voice part in 3/8 time and the right-hand melody in quasi 5/8. Its flaw is the obstreperous ending. 'Waldmädchen' (1887) was Wolf's first and unsuccessful attempt at fairy music. He omitted these last two settings and 'Die Nacht' from the revised edition of the Eichendorff volume published in 1898, as unrepresentative.

After the concentrated effort of the Mörike volume, Wolf seems to have written the majority of his twenty Eichendorff songs in a relaxed, unbuttoned state of mind. Which may partly explain why he was so strongly attracted by what may be called the poet's 'picaresque' verses, a genre to which Eichendorff's novel, *Aus dem Leben eines Taugenichts*, may also be said to belong. True, with very few exceptions, his Eichendorff collection lacks the emotional and musical weight of his other major song volumes – in later years Wolf came to consider Eichendorff's poetry somewhat superficial – but it contains settings of great zest and *joie de vivre* and displays his full command of a lighter, more diverting style.

The Goethe Songs

Johann Wolfgang von Goethe (1749–1832), poet, playwright, novelist, statesman and scientist, was really a Renaissance figure and the last universal genius Western civilisation produced. As a poet he is peerless in the wonderful interpenetration of emotion and intellect, of heart and mind, to say nothing of the enormous range of his imagination and the incomparable beauty and vividness of his verbal imagery. In his verses, notably his love lyrics, in which his only true successor was Heine, Goethe extended the evocative and expressive quality of the German language in a miraculous way. Under the influence of Herder, he came to write *Gedankenlyrik* or 'philosophical lyricism' – verses embodying his thoughts about the relationship of God, nature and man. To this genre belong 'Wanderers Nachtlied', 'Grenzen der Menschheit' and 'Prometheus', all set by Schubert and Wolf.

Goethe was for Wolf a tremendous challenge. If in his Mörike songs Wolf seemed under an irresistible compulsion to compose, in the large majority of his fifty-one Goethe settings (published in 1890) we sense a very conscious effort of the will, a flexing of all his intellectual muscles to write music worthy of the great poet. For a reason set out below, Wolf was driven to make his choice, mostly, from Goethe's lesser known, more abstract and didactic poetry and from the *Westöstlicher Divan*, and the results were songs in which pure lyricism is pressed hard to assert itself against such 'intellectual' features as harmonic-rhythmic patterns, contrast of keys and formal design. In other words, it is the more cerebral aspect of the composer's make-up that in a great number of Goethe settings comes to the fore.

It was Wolf's general maxim not to resort to poems already successfully set by previous composers, yet, when he did so, as for instance in the case of Goethe's *Wilhelm Meister* verses, 'Prometheus' or 'Grenzen der Menschheit', it implied criticism of Schubert's settings, which he thought misinterpreted Goethe's intentions. But it cannot be gainsaid that posterity on the whole still prefers the more lyrical and straightforward songs of Schubert.

The importance Wolf attached to his Harper and Mignon songs from *Wilhelm Meister* is seen from the fact that in the published collection of his Goethe settings, he placed them at the head (just as he placed the great trinity – 'Grenzen der Menschheit', 'Ganymed' and Prometheus' – at the end). He said himself that he did not simply compose the music for the Harper and Mignon verses just as they stood, but attempted to project these characters as they are described in the novel; that is, he consciously tried to bring out the pathological element in them. In order to see the Harper and Mignon in their true light, i.e. as two characters of an abnormal, unhinged mind, we have to read the novel (as Wolf did) and not confine ourselves to the verses alone, which, significantly, Goethe also published independently of the novel. The verses do not spring naturally from the novel and, though they speak most eloquently of misery, suffering, grief and despair, they do not appear as an integral part of *Wilhelm Meister* but rather as lyrical interpolations to lend the characters a more poetic dimension. It is said, indeed, that Goethe fitted the poems into the framework of the novel only with difficulty. It is therefore legitimate to argue that a composer may take either line of approach in setting these poems – in the context of the novel or outside it. Schubert certainly set them without their narrative background. Yet, we must bear in mind that the ultimate criterion of a setting is whether it is enjoyable and musically significant. And this Schubert's songs certainly are. They are inspired, very beautiful and deeply felt, and as compositions *per se* they are masterly. But they are flawed as *interpretations* of Goethe's intentions. *Per contra*, Wolf's settings, which may not always satisfy the musician in us, score the highest mark as a reflection of Goethe's implications. In projecting the abnormal traits in the two characters, Wolf probes far deeper into their psyches than any other composer who attempted to portray them. The question now arises: how is the pathological to be represented in music? How is it to be portrayed? You can do it by giving a melody and/or rhythm a strange, bizarre, *outré* shape, but, if persisted in for too long, this will defeat its own ends. It is, rather, by harmonic means – in its effect far more subliminal and, hence, more insidious than peculiar melodic and rhythmic configurations – that the pathological can best be projected. This is exactly Wolf's method, learned from Wagner's exploitation of harmony to mirror a character's deepest feelings and thoughts.[1] Wolf uses the most intense chromaticism in order to portray an unbalanced, half-crazed mind: semitonal *appoggiature*, suspensions and chromatic alterations of diatonic chords underpinning a (mostly) tortuous melody. This has a two-fold result: a considerable raising of the level of dissonance and, as a corollary, an obfuscation of tonality. As to the latter, it is especially in the Harper's songs that Wolf submerges the key-centre in a sea of chromatics as though to suggest a mind that has lost its moorings in reality. Thus, in the four-bar piano introduction to 'An die Türen will ich schleichen' and 'Wer nie sein Brot' (also in the eight-bar prelude to Mignon's 'Nur wer die Sehnsucht kennt'), it is not until the final bar that we perceive a solid tonal centre:

[1] The Strauss of *Salome* and *Elektra* and the Berg of *Wozzeck* carried this to a *ne plus ultra*.

Ex.13

Significantly, the tormented, guilt-laden sinners of the *Spanish Song Book* – in a sense also pathological characters – speak the same harmonic language as the Harper.

Wolf's three Harper settings show, in contrast to Schubert's, no indulgence in expansive, lyrical writing. Taut and concentrated, they are a compelling portrait of the old man as described in the novel – Agostino (that is his name) is completely shut in in a world of delusions and bowed down by his feeling of terrible guilt: he is, unbeknown to both, the father of Mignon, who was born of an incestuous relationship with his own sister. All three songs are (as in Schubert) in the minor and linked by a descending figure which is Wolf's symbol of deep sorrow and despair:

Ex.14 (Harfenspieler I)

Objections have been raised against Wolf's 'Wer nie sein Brot' on the grounds that, forgetting his admirable restraint and objective stance in the first two Harper settings, he introduces a startlingly violent climax at the last line, 'denn alle Schuld rächt sich auf Erden' ('for all guilt is punished on this earth'). Yet, given the tremendous emotional upsurge of Goethe's line, it would seem to demand something of a musical eruption, even at the risk of slightly unbalancing the song.

The Mignon of the novel is a truly enigmatic character. On the one hand, she is naive, innocent, trusting as a child and possessed of a most intense yearning for her native Italy ('Kennst du das Land'). On the other, she has a mysterious premonition of her early death ('So lasst mich scheinen') and is tormented by the thought that in some strange way an unspeakable tragedy is bound up with her life ('Heiss mich nicht reden'). Schubert, in his settings of the Mignon poems, by-passes this unsettling and somewhat weird element in the girl. In his conception she is an entirely child-like creature, singing of her sufferings and longings in simple, straightforward, yet nonetheless most poignant tones. Yet, if he did read the novel, he must have read it in a careless, superficial way. Not so Schumann. His Mignon is a far more complex character, as she is in the novel introvert, reflective and at the same time capable of great passion, all of which is caught in the finest of Schumann's *Wilhelm Meister* settings, 'Heiss mich nicht reden', which is a highly original creation that far surpasses both the Schubert and Wolf settings in its impact.

From a purely psychological point of view, Wolf's four Mignon songs are unquestionably most impressive, but musically 'Heiss mich nicht reden', which borrows its main rhythm from Schubert's corresponding setting, is the least successful. On the other hand, 'So lasst mich scheinen', expressing Mignon's death-wish, is treated with the utmost tenderness, the music radiating the ineffable beauty of disembodied, immaterial things. It is only once, at the climax of the last line, that the otherwise muted dynamics rise to a *forte*. Entirely *sui generis* is 'Nur wer die Sehnsucht kennt', which we shall fully appreciate only if we banish from our minds the expansive, melancholy phrases of the Schubert song. The melodic interest in the Wolf piece is small and the instrumental texture unchanging, yet what wonderful plasticity and liquescence in the declamatory line! Add Wolf's rubato style and you have the merely technical basis of a song most deeply stirring in its evocation of loneliness and unstilled longing. In this setting of fifty-seven bars, the tonic chord of G minor is touched but once, and then only as an unstressed passing-note harmony near the end.

Perhaps the most celebrated of the *Wilhelm Meister* poems is Mignon's 'Kennst du das Land', in which Goethe expresses the Northerner's eternal longing for the sunbathed, radiant South. The poem has been set to music countless times, but whether ever perfectly remains a moot question. The reason for this lies not in the verses themselves but in the way the Mignon of the novel sings it to her friend and protector, Wilhelm Meister. As Goethe describes it, in her delivery of the words Mignon changes her expression constantly – from a measured solemnity in the opening to gloom in the third line, to an irresistible yearning in the refrain, 'Dahin, dahin!...'

which she modifies in each of its repetitions, making it sound now urgent and pleading, now compelling and full of passion. Reading Goethe's description of Mignon's delivery, no setting is likely to satisfy the critical listener completely. For to recapture, within the limitations of a song, *all* Mignon's swiftly changing moods and yet preserve musical unity would seem a well-nigh impossible task. Of all the composers known to me who attempted a setting of 'Kennst du das Land', Wolf comes nearest to achieving it; which is the more remarkable since the song is cast into a merely slightly varied strophic mould. Yet in depicting the pathological in Mignon, he portrays her in a crescendo of febrile, almost hysterical excitement, e.g. the recurring piano phrase of descending octaves (bar 21 *et passim*) and the rise of the voice, at her outcry, 'Dahin, dahin!', from E flat to G flat and A flat above the stave. Wolf's conception of Mignon is worlds apart from Schubert's, in which she appears as a child singing longingly yet with joyful expectation of her motherland. The Wolfian Mignon is too grown-up, too neurotic, and tormented, almost to the point of self-laceration, by her yearning for a land of dreams which, we know, will never become reality.

We now turn to the last three songs of Wolf's Goethe volume. Given the composer's total identification with the mood, imagery and meaning of a poem, it is not surprising to encounter in 'Prometheus', 'Ganymed' and 'Grenzen der Menschheit' a markedly different style from that of the Harper and Mignon settings; their intense chromaticism now yields to a more 'healthy' diatonic writing.

Prometheus is the great rebel of ancient Greek mythology and in his poem, one of his grandest and most powerful conceptions, Goethe identifies with him, throwing out his challenge to the gods and proclaiming his unshakeable confidence in the strength of his own genius. Wolf's setting is, like Schubert's (an equally resplendent but less imperious song), cast as a dramatic *scena*, which captures most impressively Prometheus's defiance and arrogant pride. In the twenty-two bars of the piano prelude, Wolf exposes almost the entire material of the composition, thus ensuring a measure of musical coherence and unity missing from Schubert's more rhapsodic treatment, with its division into recitative, arioso and closed form. The Wagnerian influence can be detected in the monumental scale of the setting and, more particularly, in the Wotanesque theme of mightily rising piano octaves at 'musst mir mein Erde doch lassen' ('but you cannot touch my world'). The setting cries out for an orchestral version of the accompaniment, which Wolf later provided but which suffers from over-scoring.[1]

If Goethe's 'Prometheus' expresses man's rebellion against the gods, its opposite, 'Grenzen der Menschheit', conveys man's sense of humility and insignificance before the omnipotence of divine power. Schubert's setting has majesty and grandeur, Wolf's awe and submission. It follows a pictorial path in such suggestive word-paintings as the strong, sturdy march tune at 'Steht er mit festen markigen Knochen' ('if he stand strong and firm . . .') and the billowing figures at 'Dass viele Wellen wandeln . . .' ('that many waves roll on . . .'). In addition, Wolf employs a constructive rhythm as characterising symbol, such as even minims for the majesty of the gods and even crotchets for the insignificance of man.[2] In 'Ganymed' Goethe resorts to another legend of Greek mythology, according to which Ganymede, a Phrygian youth of surpassing beauty, was borne up to heaven to serve as cupbearer for Zeus and the other gods. Goethe interprets it in a highly original manner, namely as an expression of a deep-rooted longing for mystic union with God and nature, springing from the poet's own pantheistic leanings. This longing, conveyed by Wolf for the most part in muted, subdued tones, is the key-note of his setting, which shows a rare three-bar structure at the opening and later. It is a finely-wrought setting, and notable for the poetic effect derived from Wolf's mediant key-shifts. Yet there are musicians who prefer Schubert's more extrovert song: not only on account of its greater wealth of melodies but also because its dynamic, through-composed form accords better with the *evolving* character of the poem than Wolf's closed A-B-A scheme.

One of the most memorable of Wolf's remaining Goethe settings is 'Anakreons Grab', perhaps the paradigm of Wolf's objective treatment. Mood, imagery and meaning are completely absorbed into the music, and yet you feel that the individuality of the verses remains as intact as if they were recited. It is almost a case of the poet becoming the musician. In its mixture of muted serenity and wist-

[1] The only performance I have heard of the original version that did full justice to Wolf's grandiose conception was one given by Dietrich Fischer-Dieskau, with Rudolf Sawallisch at the piano, at the Royal Albert Hall some years ago.

[2] Sams furnishes a list of such constructive rhythmic patterns used by Wolf in the song, *op. cit.*, p. 161.

fulness, Wolf's setting has something in common with Brahms's 'Feldeinsamkeit'. The declamation of the text is a study in itself. Two examples may suffice. Note the contrast in the setting of the antithesis of 'Grab' and 'Leben', the first on a short low F and the second on the sustained D, a sixth higher; while the pause Wolf inserts between 'Es ist' – Anakreons Ruh' most subtly heightens the effect of the second half of the phrase. Significantly, Wolf reduces the chromatic harmony to a diatonic G major on 'Ruh'. The extremely beautiful postlude is like the evocation of a sunset in a classical landscape.

'Blumengruss', which in the accompaniment pays tribute to Schubert's 'Geheimes', and 'Gleich und Gleich' are ravishingly beautiful flower songs, foreshadowing settings in the *Spanish* and *Italian Song Books*. 'Frühling übers Jahr', with its bell-like accompaniment, is a love song full of the ineffable fragrance of a spring morning. There is deliberate irony behind Goethe's two mock-pastorals, 'Die Spröde' and 'Die Bekehrte'. The verses tell of a shepherdess who, in the first poem, coquettishly rejects a lover's tempting advances while, in the second, having yielded to him, she laments his desertion of her. (The text reads like a parody of Gretchen's 'Meine Ruh ist hin, mein Herz ist schwer'.) Of the two settings, 'Die Bekehrte', with its suggestions of the shepherd's (Damon) flute, of occasional bagpipe drones, and with the augmented fourth prominent, is the more exquisite.

'Epiphanias' was written for the celebration of Melanie Köchert's birthday on Epiphany 1888, when it was sung and acted in costume by her three children. It combines in an entrancing way mock-solemnity and child-like humour. The Three Kings arrive and depart with a collective theme of a processional character, but, in addition, each has a melody of his own, the most delightful of which is the *alla turca* characterising the black king. 'Sankt Nepomuks Vorabend', the verses of which are based on legend associated with the martyrdom of Bohemia's patron saint, is a song of pervasive tenderness, with the high-lying accompaniment evoking the sound of soft, ethereal bells. Of Wolf's Goethe ballads, 'Ritter Kurts Brautfahrt' and 'Gutmann und Gutweib' are comparative failures: there is too much detailed musical commentary and no single plain statement projected in terms of an alluring melody. But 'Der Rattenfänger' is a most brilliant *tour de force* in a breathtaking tarantella rhythm. It is one of Wolf's most popular Goethe settings.

As already remarked, in his search for Goethe poems not previously set by Schubert and Schumann, Wolf was driven to look farther afield, selecting verses that did not naturally lend themselves to musical treatment. There is, therefore, something forced and contrived about such settings as 'Frech und Froh' I and II, 'Genialisch Treiben' and songs based on poems of philosophical wisdoms and didactic maxims, like 'Cophtisches Lied' I and II and 'Beherzigung'. But none is negligible, especially not the first of the Coptic settings, with its ironic refrain. But considering the nature of the verses the real Wolfian afflatus is, not unexpectedly, missing. Much the same may be said of many of Wolf's seventeen settings from the *Westöstlicher Divan* – a collection of orientalising poems[1] modelled by Goethe on the fourteenth-century Persian poet Hafiz, to which he was inspired by his love for the young Marianne von Willemer.

One of Wolf's finest and most interesting settings here is 'Phänomen', to a poem from the section *Buch des Sängers*. The phenomenon of the title is the multicoloured rainbow ingeniously mirrored in a constant change of harmonic colours. In a song of sixteen bars, almost every key is touched, yet without ever creating the impression of being contrived or *voulu*. Another section from the above collection is *Schenkenbuch*, an encomium on the blissful, intoxicating power of the grape. (Baudelaire's five poems 'Le Vin' in his *Fleurs du mal* are of similar intent; three of them were set by Berg in his concert aria 'Der Wein'.) Wolf's settings do full justice to the verses of the drunken philosopher as far as voice and piano can be made to do it, but in the process songs like the bacchanalian 'Trunken müssen wir alle sein!' and the furiously driving 'Wenn in der Schenke' (a setting not dissimilar to 'Genialisch Treiben') go beyond the notion of the traditional *Lied*. They are 'characteristic' songs which, we presume, accorded well with the 'wild' Wolf. Singer and pianist here have to display a maximum of virtuosity. Perhaps Wolf's most successful settings are those to verses in the section, *Buch der Suleika*, to which Marianne von Willemer contributed three lyrics. (Two of these were set by Schubert in his splendid 'Suleika' songs; Marianne was also the author of 'Versunken' in the

[1] In this context Goethe himself might be quoted who in a letter to Zelter (11 March 1816) wrote that the form of poetry he adopted in his *Westöstlicher Divan* has 'the peculiarity that, almost like the sonnet, it is unsuitable for singing' – a fact Wolf disregarded, not always to his advantage.

Buch der Liebe.) Goethe and Marianne appear as Hatem and Suleika, both expressing their love in terms of rich Eastern imagery. There is a dichotomy in Wolf's ten settings. On the one hand, you find songs of unconstrained, flaming passion like 'Hochbeglückt', 'Locken, haltet mich gefangen' and 'Nimmer will ich dich verlieren', and, on the other, songs of a more inward, contemplative character, such as the dreamlike 'Wie sollt ich heiter bleiben' and its companion piece 'Wenn ich dein gedenke'. Outstanding among the songs of this group is the verbally and thematically related pair, 'Als ich auf dem Euphrat schiffte' and 'Dies zu deuten bin erbötig', the first a woman's song (Suleika) and the second sung by a man (Hatem). The dream of drifting on the river is most suggestively caught in the tender barcarolle-like movement of the former, with the girl's question, 'Sag, Prophete! Was bedeutet dieser Traum?' ('Tell me, prophet! What does this dream mean?') ending on the dominant; note also the unusual phrasing of the voice part: 5 plus 3 plus 4 plus 5 bars. In contrast, the lover's interpretation of the dream is given in the latter song in forceful, animated language.

The Spanish Song Book

The poems of the *Spanish Song Book* (published in 1891) derive from a collection of sixteenth- and seventeenth-century verse in a translation (published in 1852) by Paul Heyse and Emanuel Geibel. About half are by anonymous authors and the rest by such writers as Cervantes, Lope de Vega and Camoens. What was it that made Wolf resort to this collection, which is transmitted poetry, at one remove from the original, and rendered by two different authors? There are two main reasons for this. The first and general is that Wolf, alone among the great German songwriters, was most strongly attracted to the spirit and landscape of a Mediterranean of the mind, just as his contemporary Nietzsche was. The rich fruit of this was the *Spanish Song Book*, the opera *Der Corregidor*, the operatic fragment *Manuel Venegas*, and the Italian songs. Secondly, with his Goethe settings Wolf had, as it were, used up German poetry of the quality he demanded of his poets and, probably spurred on by Schumann's and Brahms's examples, turned to these translations from the Spanish. The fact that they were translations seems to have determined Wolf's musical approach to them. It is no longer the words as such, as in Mörike and Goethe, that provided the immediate inspiration, but rather the ideas, concepts and moods underlying the poems on which he now concentrated. This distancing from the verbal poetry of a lyric resulted in Wolf liberating himself from his previous faithful and scrupulous submission to the poet, and allowed him to give his purely musical impulses freer rein than before. The dominating features of the Spanish songs are rhythm, especially dance rhythms, guitar figures in the accompaniment, recurring refrains, harmony and formal design, while the purely melodic interest moves into the background. Following Heyse and Geibel, Wolf divided his Spanish volume into *Geistliche Gesänge* (10) and *Weltliche Gesänge* (34), most of the latter being love songs, on which he imprinted his personality with intensity and subjective self-expression. An objective stance is adopted only in the religious settings.

The first six of the ten sacred songs form a group insofar as they all radiate extreme gentleness and sublime simplicity of feeling. Three are outstandingly fine. In 'Die ihr schwebet' the Virgin beseeches the angels to guard her child against the cold winds blowing over the palm tree under which she has sought shelter. A four-bar ostinato in the accompaniment is made to do service for various verbal images and Wolf most aptly employs mediant key-shifts and dynamic modifications to fit the Virgin's changing mood. (Brahms's setting of the same poem, 'Geistliches Wiegenlied', for contralto, piano and viola obbligato, is of a more veiled beauty.) In 'Nun wandre, Maria', the Virgin and Joseph trudge their way to Bethlehem, the solicitous husband comforting his pregnant spouse over the arduousness of their journey. Their regular, plodding steps are graphically caught in the uninterrupted quaver movements up and down the scale in the piano's right hand, its thirds standing for close companionship. Similarly characterised is the beautiful 'Führ mich, Kind, nach Bethlehem', the accompaniment of which Wolf described as being like a four-part chorus. In strongest contrast to this is the mood of the last four sacred songs, which is one of abject contrition and remorse, the sinner praying to the Virgin and Christ to redeem his soul from eternal damnation. A salient feature of these settings is Wolf's adherence throughout, literally or in slight variation, to an identical piano figure, suggesting that his ostinato here has the symbolic meaning of the sinner's almost pathological obsession with his guilt. The resulting monotony is deliberate and designed to produce a hypnotic effect. Chromatic harmony, often leading to grinding dissonances and the veiling of the true tonality, as shown in Ex. 15 from 'Herr, was trägt der Boden hier', are additional means to convey an abnormal degree of self-torment:

Ex.15

The vocal line tends, significantly, to move in small intervals, recalling Gregorian chant. All four settings are highly original in conception and two of them – 'Herr, was trägt der Boden hier' and 'Wunden trägst du', both of which represent a dialogue between the sinner and the Saviour – are masterpieces.

The secular songs of the Spanish volume portray erotic love in its diverse moods – bliss and unhappiness, torment and rapture, despair and mockery. It is a most vivid series of vignettes of men and women caught in the eternal war of the sexes, which is particularly fierce in Southern countries. Like Schumann and Jensen in *their* settings from Heyse's and Geibel's collection, Wolf introduces local colour by means of guitar effects and quasi-Spanish dance rhythms which add to the appeal of the more light-hearted songs, but seem somewhat contrived and superfluous in the serious settings. The new style of the Spanish songs is felt in the increased flexibility of the voice part, sometimes at the expense of correct declamation, in an added rhythmic brilliance and in the treatment of the accompaniment as almost a piano solo.[1] This seems to have been Wolf's primary conception to which the voice part was subsequently added.

This section of the *Spanish Song Book* opens with the dance-song, 'Klinge, klinge, mein Pandero', in which a girl tries to drown her sorrows of love in a dance accompanied by the tinkle of a tambourine. It is not a great song but a good illustration of Wolf's sense of dramatic irony, which lies in the contrast between the girl's despairing words and the brilliance of her gay dance. The song recalls a similar emotional situation in Wolf's early Heine setting, 'Sie haben heut Abend Gesellschaft'. 'In dem Schatten meiner Locken' is justly a great favourite, partly for its delightful poem and

[1] 'Klinge, klinge, mein Pandero', 'Auf dem grünen Balkon', 'Bitt'ihn, o Mutter!'

largely for its most felicitous setting. The girl's lover has fallen asleep in the shadow of her tresses, and in an insinuating mixture of tender love, affection and coquettishness she asks whether she should wake him up – despite the fact that he calls her his tormentor and yet has gone to sleep by her side. The music is drenched in sunshine, and combines invention and technical *savoir faire* to produce a song full of enchantment and delicate charm. Wolf may have read into the poem more psychological subtleties than it actually contains, and hence the many pointed mediant shifts and dynamic changes. Note also the treatment of her delightful phrase, 'Weck' ich ihn nun auf? Ach nein!' ('Shall I wake him? Ah, no!'); the question ending on a rising interval (fourth, sixth) and the answer on a falling third.[1] There follows a group of songs for male voice, in which the lover laments, humorously or in bitterness, the fickleness and cruelty of his sweetheart. Easily the finest among them is 'Auf dèm grünen Balkon', in which a lover complains that his girl on the balcony, while luring him on with her eyes, says 'no' with a gesture of her finger. Wolf has rarely hit upon two more felicitous piano themes than those in A major and C sharp minor which wed an irresistible rhythmic lilt to infinite melodic charm, the entire serenade being sung above strumming guitar chords in the bass. Add to this the subtle handling of the thrice-repeated 'nein!', the successive settings of which seem to imply a gradual lessening of the girl's resistance, and the perfection of this song is clear. Both 'Seltsam ist Juanas Weise' and 'Treibe nur mit Lieben Spott' have a recurring refrain – '"Morgen," sagt sie leise' ('"Tomorrow," she murmurs softly') in the first is particularly expressive – and are in the minor. These two characteristics hold good also for other male songs, such as the passionate 'Blindes Schauen', in which the text is a succession of oxymora ('Blindes Schauen, dunkle Leuchte, Ruhm voll Weh' – 'Blind yet seeing, dark yet shining, glory yet sorrows'); the ironic 'Eide, so die Liebe schwur' and 'Herz, verzage nicht', which in a nutshell contains the moral of Mozart's *Così fan tutte*. The delightful refrain of the last song, 'Weil die Weiber Weiber sind' ('because women will be women') occurs five times, three times differently set, suggesting the lover's changing stance in propounding this perennial wisdom.

[1] Wolf later incorporated this song into Act I of *Der Corregidor* where it is sung by the miller's wife, Frasquita. It has, regrettably, totally eclipsed Brahms's exquisite setting.

One would not be surprised if one had come across the adorable 'Wenn du zu den Blumen gehst' among the Mörike or Goethe songs. There is nothing even faintly Spanish about it, on the contrary it is a most heart-felt and tender German love-song, Schumannesque in its vocal melody and Bachian in the piano part. Its central idea – that the sweetheart's beauty surpasses that of every flower in the garden – as well as its home key (A major) at once recall the Goethe setting, 'Frühling übers Jahr'. The humorously sad counterpart to the Spanish song is 'Wer sein holdes Lieb verloren', which is about an exceptionally timid lover who fails to take appropriate advantage of the girl sinking down among the flowers of the garden. Thematic resemblance between the openings and key relationship (major and relative minor) as well as order of sequence make it almost certain that Wolf intended the second song as a sequel to the first. Incidentally, Wolf scored both settings for inclusion in his operatic fragment, *Manuel Venegas*.

It is, perhaps, significant that the secular part of the *Spanish Song Book* contains only eight women's songs as against more than three times as many men's songs. A few are of a humorous character, such as the mocking 'Sagt, seid Ihr es, feiner Herr' and 'Mögen alle bösen Zungen', in which the chatter of evil tongues is delightfully recaptured in both the voice and piano parts. Of serious intent is the impassioned 'Sagt ihm, dass er zu mir komme', whose key of B minor Wolf seems to have associated (as in 'Blindes Schauen' and 'Eide so die Liebe schwur') with a bitter-sweet sentiment. Characteristic of the prevalent mood is the marking *Leidenschaftlich* (passionately) of 'Liebe mir im Busen zündet' and 'Schmerzliche Wonnen', both in the manner of a tearaway tarantella, as is also the coruscating 'Wer tat deinem Füsslein weh?' An outstanding example of Wolf at his inventive best is 'Trau nicht der Liebe', which captures the blend of wistfulness and irony most felicitously. It is a *siciliano* in A minor, with the voice and the piano going their separate ways yet creating a sense of complete unity of conception. There are entrancing illustrative touches such as the descending staccato quavers of the instrument which continue into the refrain's last line, 'Wo du heut' gelacht' ('Where you laughed today'). This is another song that shows a striking affinity in mood, key, texture, down even to a little piano figure, and tempo with 'Die Bekehrte' in the Goethe volume. Provided we seek for no connection whatever between words and music – rare in Wolf – the song, 'Ach, im Maien wars' must be accounted a gem, with a beautiful shape of the *cantabile* voice part and the lilting guitar accompaniment, the latter pointing forward to the entrancing 'Ein Ständchen euch zu bringen' in the Italian songs. Wolf may have interpreted the anonymous text as a traditional ancient Romance and set it accordingly.

A small group of songs in a most deeply-felt melancholy vein includes 'Alle gingen, Herz, zur Ruh', which compresses a whole interior drama into no more than twenty bars; it would not be amiss in the Mörike volume. Wolf suggests the beat of the wounded heart in a syncopated bass figure which goes almost throughout the setting. The emotional curve of the music is $\smile$ *ff* $\frown$, with, perhaps, too excessive a climax (*fortissimo* in the piano) in a setting of predominantly muted dynamics. 'Dereinst, dereinst, Gedanke mein', 'Tief im Herzen trag ich Pein' and 'Komm, o Tod, von Nacht umgeben' recall in their sentiment those guilt-laden sinners of the sacred Spanish songs. The last two show features similar to those settings – intense chromaticism and blurred tonality. The finest of these four songs is, perhaps, 'Komm, o Tod' in C minor, in which the accompaniment unfolds in the manner of a grave sarabande – note the recurring stress on the second beat of every bar. An aspect of this plainly self-torturing mood is displayed in the exquisite love-song, 'Bedeckt mich mit Blumen', in which a lover who is dying for love asks that his body be covered in flowers. Wolf responds to this in music of quiet rapture, with a delicate, pliable vocal line floating above a Schumannesque accompaniment that is dominated by the composer's 'yearning' figure (Ex. 9b), best known from 'Auf einer Wanderung' in the Mörike songs.

The crowning glory of the *Spanish Song Book* is 'Geh, Geliebter, geh jetzt!', which is about a girl bidding farewell to her lover after a night of passionate embraces. A dramatic *scena* (as are most of Wolf's dramatic lyrical miniatures) rather than a song, it has a magnificent sweep and grandeur and most intense feeling. It is an illustration of Wolf's autonomous 'symphonic' writing at its most impressive, with the instrumental part being central in suggesting the slight yet noticeable changes in the situation, and greatly adding to the urgency of the voice part. The swaying, long-breathed line of the opening (Ex. 16) is one of Wolf's finest vocal inspirations.

It recurs three more times as the refrain of the song but it can also be interpreted as the ritornello in a rondo with three episodes; the second and third episodes, both in E major in a song in F sharp

Ex.16

Geh,____ Ge - lieb - ter, geh jetzt! ____

Sieh' der Mor - gen däm - - mert.

major, introduce some new material. Interestingly enough, Wolf uses at the passage 'Wenn die Sonn'am Himmel scheinend' ('When the sun is shining in the sky') an *espressivo* piano figure closely akin to the motive at 'Ach hier, wie liegt die Welt so licht' ('Oh, how bright is here the world') (Ex. 9b) in the Mörike song 'Auf einer Wanderung'. The musical affinity is explained by the similarity of the verbal images, both suggesting 'brightness' as a symbol of happiness or bliss. Still more striking is the similarity between 'Geh, Geliebter, geh jetzt!' and Mignon's 'Kennst du das Land', both settings sharing the same key, time-signature $(9/8 = 3/4)$, the *tempo rubato* and the symphonic role of the accompaniment. It would be idle to speculate on rational reasons for this strong resemblance except to say that the feeling behind 'Geh, Geliebter, geh jetzt!' may have unconsciously recalled to Wolf the sentiment behind the phrase 'Dahin, dahin, möcht' ich mit dir, mein Geliebter, ziehn!' in the Goethe setting. No doubt, the theme of the Spanish song – secret and illicit love – must have struck a deep chord in Wolf, the lover of Melanie Köchert, which explains perhaps the extraordinary intensity of the music. And he knew why he placed this song at the end of his published volume of Spanish songs. Incidentally, the composer omitted one stanza from the original poem, just as he added one to 'Benedeit die sel'ge Mutter' in the *Italian Song Book*.

A certain number of the Spanish songs are, admittedly, uneven in invention and/or treatment, and this applies in particular to some not mentioned hitherto in this chapter. One appreciates the advice given by Wolf's publishers (Schott) to select for publication only the songs of outstanding artistic merit, an advice Wolf did not take. But this comparative failure must be blamed largely on the relevant lyrics, which failed, either totally or intermittently, to kindle Wolf's imagination ('Ich fuhr über Meer', 'Schmerzliche Wonnen', 'Deine

Mutter, süsses Kind', and so on). Others again ('Bitt'ihn, o Mutter', 'Wehe der, die mir verstrickte meinen Geliebten!') make their effect less by the intrinsic quality of the music than by the choice of singer, who must be a soprano of true dramatic thrust and with a reliable top register. Yet this in no way detracts from the fact that, besides containing a small handful of masterpieces, the *Spanish Song Book*, considered as a whole, represents an important change of direction in Wolf's setting of a text and, hence, in style, the full import of which will be seen in the Italian song volume.

The Keller Songs
The Italian Song Book

Gottfried Keller (1819–90) was Switzerland's most important nineteenth-century writer, and his great novel, *Der grüne Heinrich*, was one of Wolf's favourites. He intended his *Alte Weisen (Old Tunes)*, six settings of verses by Keller, published in 1891, as a tribute for the poet's seventieth birthday, but the latter died before the completion of the set. Significantly, Wolf experienced, against his expectation, difficulties with the composition, difficulties that were largely due to the fact that in these songs he was trying to go, as it were, against his grain and reverse the new direction in which his own development had been moving in the Spanish volume. The word becomes again the source of inspiration and there is a noticeable return to the type of character sketch ('Tretet ein, hoher Krieger!', 'Das Köhlerweib ist trunken') exemplified in some of the Eichendorff settings. In addition, we notice a sagging of invention. Yet there is an unquestionable masterpiece among the six *Old Tunes* – 'Wie glänzt der helle Mond', which is in general character reminiscent of the music of the early Heine song, 'Wie des Mondes Abbild zittert', and the later 'Der Mond hat eine schwere Klag'erhoben'. It is a setting of the utmost tenderness and sensitivity, cast in A-B-A form, which does not quite harmonise with the developing tale of the poem. The harmonic adventurousness of 'Du milchjunger Knabe' is particularly striking, while 'Wandl'ich in dem Morgentau' has an engaging freshness and flow; its accompaniment reiterates the same figure in constant melodic and harmonic variations throughout the whole song. 'Das Köhlerweib ist trunken' begins splendidly with a graphic evocation in the piano part of the charcoaler's drunken wife bawling through the woods. It might have become an outstanding song had not Wolf by-passed the meaning of the further lines which relate how she was once the belle of the region and how transitory mortal beauty is. The song conveys nothing but mockery and scorn.

'My Italian songs are the most original and artistically the most perfect of all my things', wrote Wolf in a letter of December 1891. His instinct was right. For felicity of invention, delicate and limpid beauty and technical refinement, the large majority of these settings stand in a class of their own, adding a new, precious jewel to the crown of the German *Lied*. Part I appeared in 1892 and Part II in 1896. As with his previous great collections, a new kind of literary stimulus brought forth from Wolf a *seemingly* new musical style, thus revealing a new facet of his protean genius. I say 'seemingly' – since Wolf continued in fact to move further in the new direction he had taken in the *Spanish Song Book* and reached a new peak of consummation in the creation of lyrical miniatures. All the poems of the Italian songs are anonymous, all are love-poems and all have the same translator, which makes for a unified and fully integrated literary style, yet without a strong creative personality to direct them. The corollary is that, more than in his Spanish volume, Wolf the musician came to the fore and, no longer under the self-denying ordinance of surrendering wholly to the poet, was able to permeate the music with his personality. What with that, their brevity and their peculiar metrical patterns, the Italian volume has been declared, not without some exaggeration, when we think of the many masterpieces in the Mörike and Goethe settings, as the finest of his collections.

In these songs we notice a greater directness of utterance and emotional immediacy, a new clarity and simplicity in the melodic and harmonic language and a 'lean', slimmed-down texture, all of which would seem to constitute the Italian dimension in these otherwise German creations (see p. 55). But there is scarcely any suggestion of local colour. Except for an occasional hint of a guitar or lute ('Ein Ständchen euch zu bringen'), Wolf makes no attempt to unfurl a national flag as he does so assiduously in his Spanish songs. Some settings show a curious detachment of the music from the verses ('Und steht Ihr früh am Morgen auf', 'Ich liess mir sagen', 'O wüsstest du'), in which the two seem to inhabit different worlds that refuse to merge. Others again display a more contrapuntal, string-quartet writing in the accompaniment ('Was für ein Lied', 'Wohl kenn'ich Euren Stand', 'Nicht länger kann ich singen', all dating from 1896). This is what Wolf described as his 'absolute music', which is an odd description for a composer whose imagination was so markedly dependent on extra-musical, literary incentives in order to be able to work at full stretch.

The *Italian Song Book* comprises forty-six songs, composed in three bouts of feverish creativity between September 1890 and April 1896. The first bout occurred between 25 September and 13 November 1890, when Wolf wrote seven songs of which 'Mir ward gesagt' was the first. Then, after a full year's interruption, during which Wolf was in despair at his creative silence, followed the next fifteen songs, composed between 29 November and 23 December 1891. There followed another and this time extra-ordinarily long interval of four years up to 1895, the year of *Der Corregidor*, and the last twenty-four songs were put on paper in scarcely more than a month – 25 March to 30 April 1896. Wolf's remarkable feat resides in the fact that when he took up again where he had left off, he continued in exactly the same style and manner of the first half of songs written four to five years before, though one or the other of the 1896 settings may have been composed, or, at any rate, sketched earlier and subsequently revised. In any case, the absence of a stylistic break argues a high degree of artistic self-discipline and control. Yet it must be added that, while Part I (1890–91) demonstrates an almost uninterrupted succession of masterly songs, Part II (1896) is flawed here and there by sagging inspiration and reliance on Wolfian formulae.

Wolf took the poems from Paul Heyse's collection, *Italienisches Liederbuch* (1860), a translation of popular Italian verses comprising ballads, death-laments, Corsican and Dalmatian songs, *ritornelli* and Tuscan (*rispetti*) and Venetian (*vilote*) love-poems. The last two are regional variants of the courtly classical *strambotto*, dating back to the fifteenth century if not earlier, and Wolf's selection was made exclusively from the *rispetti* (40) and *vilote* (5), the single exception being a Venetian folksong. These verses express a gamut of erotic emotions, from the gallant and courtly to searing passion, sadness and mocking despair. They were published around the mid-nineteenth century when they were grouped under such headings as: *Bontà e Bellezza di Donna* ('Goodness and Beauty of Woman'),

Lontananza ('Absence'), *Noncuranza e Distacco* ('Indifference and Separation'), *Innamoramento* ('Falling in Love'), *Castigo* ('Punishment'), *Preghiere e Rimproveri* ('Prayers and Reproaches'), *Canti* and *Serenate*. As always with demotic verse, the *rispetti* and *vilote* are marked by simplicity and immediacy of expression, strength of feeling and naive spontaneity.

Typical of the verse form is the single stanza consisting of, mostly, eight end-stopped lines, less frequently of six, and occasionally of twelve or more lines, as for instance the *vilota* of Wolf's 'Geselle, woll'n wir uns in Kutten hüllen' ('Compagno mio, vustu che andremo frate'). Each line has ten or eleven syllables and the rhyme-scheme favours patterns such as ababccdd or ababccaa, and with few exceptions, Heyse faithfully reproduced this scheme in his translations. Wolf, accordingly, resorts to balancing two-bar phrases in his settings, a pair of vocal phrases embracing a couplet. The single-stanza form results in songs of remarkable brevity and concentration: out of forty-six settings, only six extend to three pages, while the majority occupy two pages, and two songs a single page ('Heut Nacht erhob ich mich', 'Nicht länger kann ich singen'). A feature of these verses is their predilection for repeating the same thought in slight variations. Take, for instance, 'Heb'auf dein blondes Haupt'. No one of the 'four weighty matters' the mistress tells her lover about is of more importance than the others – all four convey to him the same message: I love you.

Alza la bionda testa, e non dormire,	Heb'auf dein blondes Haupt und schlafe nicht,
Non ti lasciar superar dallo sonno.	Und lass dich ja von Schlummer nicht betören,
Quattro parole, amore, io son per dire,	Ich sage die vier Worte von Gewicht,
Che tutte e quattro son di gran bisogno:	Von denen darfts du keines überhören.
La prima ell'è che mi fate morire,	Das erste: dass um dich mein Herze bricht,
E la seconda, che un gran ben ti voglio:	Das zweite: dir nur will'ich angehören
La terza, che vi sia raccomandata;	Das dritte: dass ich dir mein Heil befehle,
L'ultima, che di voi so' innamorata.	Das letzte: dich allein liebt meine Seele.

There is no real climax in that poem and Wolf, accordingly, sets it in a mood of unvarying tenderness and intimacy. Closely linked to this variation of the same thought is the reiteration of lines in which words are transposed and/or only slightly varied. Heyse, however, treats this with some freedom, as a comparison of the original and his translation, 'Und weil ich dich geliebt' shows:

E per amarvi voi, fresco bel viso,	Und weil ich dich geliebt, schön frisch Gesicht
Io mi ritrovo fuor del paradiso	Verschert'ich mir des Paradieses Licht
E per amarvi voi, fresca viola,	Und weil ich dich geliebt, schön Veigelein,
Del paradiso mi ritrovo fuori.	Komm'ich nun nicht ins Paradies hinein.

In some verses Heyse succeeds in heightening the comic situation considerably, as in 'Mein Liebster ist so klein':

E maledico le mosche e i cugini,	Verwünscht sei'n alle Fliegen, Schnacken, Mücken,
E chi s'innamorò de' piccolini.	Und wer sich, wenn er küsst, zu tief muss bücken.

In the accompaniment of these last two lines, Wolf amusingly suggests how the mistress has to bend down low to her minuscule lover, but in the postlude he pictures also the lover straining up to reach the girl's lips. On the whole, Heyse recaptures the flavour and atmosphere of the Italian verses admirably yet in the process he often intensifies their mood. Compare, for instance, the third line in the Italian original and in his translation, 'Heut Nacht erhob ich mich':

E io gli dissi: cor, dove vai?	Ich frug: Herz, wohin stürmst du so mit Macht?

By transforming the simple question into an anguished outcry, Heyse creates a dramatic climax absent from the original, and Wolf mirrors this accurately by allowing the vocal line to rise up to F, significantly the highest note of the song, and supporting it in the accompaniment by a crescendo to *forte*, with a six-note chord on 'Macht'. This intensification of expression results in a much-raised emotional temperature, as seen on a larger scale in, for example, 'Der Mond hat eine schwere Klag'erhoben' and 'Benedeit die sel'ge Mutter' (middle stanza), and represents the German element of Heyse's translation. In this context it is interesting to read what Wolf wrote to a friend (Kauffmann) about his settings of the *Italian Song Book*:

A warm heart, I can assure you, beats in the little bodies of my youngest children of the South, who, in spite of all, cannot deny their German origin. Yes, their heart-beat is German, even if the sun shines 'in Italian'.

In the serious love-songs we find a typically German *Innigkeit* and depth of feeling unknown to the anonymous authors of the Italian verses. It was these two factors – their anonymity and the fact that they are not great poetry – that seem to have freed Wolf from the necessity of setting the text with the same self-effacing devotion and faithfulness with which he treated the lyrics of Mörike and Goethe. He now allowed his imagination to play on the text without let or hindrance. In some cases, this amounted to a plain misreading of a poem, but it was an inspired misreading to which we owe some of the finest and psychologically most subtle character sketches and mood-pictures in the German *Lied*. Wolf introduces shades of feeling and meaning into his music that never occurred to the unknown writers of the original poems or their sophisticated and polished translator. (Significantly, Heyse is said to have cared little for Wolf's Italian songs though he greatly admired his other settings.) Take, for example, the song 'Wer rief dich denn?' As the text stands, it is all an expression of jealousy and scorn, felt by the betrayed mistress for her faithless lover:

Chi ti ci fa venir, chi ti chiama?	Wer rief dich denn? Wer hat dich herbestellt?
Chi ti ci fa venir mal volontieri?	Wer hiess dich kommen, wenn es dir zur Last?
Vanne pure dov'hai fissa la dama,	Geh zu dem Liebchen, das dir mehr gefällt,
Vanne pure dov'hai fissi i pensieri,	Geh dahin, wo du deine Gedanken hast.
Vanne pure dov'hai il pensier sicuro:	Geh nur, wohin dein Sinnen steht und Denken,
Che tu venga da me non me ne curo,	Dass du zu mir kommst, will ich gern dir schenken.
Vanne pure dov'hai fissa la dama.	Geh zu dem Liebchen, das dir mehr gefällt!
Chi ti ci fa venir? Chi ti ci chiama?	Wer rief dich denn? Wer hat dich herbestellt?

Wolf's setting is in the form of a dramatic recitative, a kind of *recitativo accompagnato*, in which he omits the balancing phrase structure so as to project the emotional drama with more immediacy. Yet there are tempo modifications, changes of dynamics, and sudden leaps of the voice to the low register, which are all tell-tale signs of an undercurrent of feeling that seem to belie the girl's fury. Note the 'zurückhaltend' ('slowing down') in bars 6 and 9 and the 'ein wenig zögernd' ('a little hesitantly') in bar 15, with the relevant vocal phrases all sung softly. Furthermore, there is in the vocal line an unexpected skip of an octave at 'Wer liess dich kommen, *wenn* es dir Last?' ('Who called you here, *if* it is a burden to you?'); a descent, by way of an augmented fifth, from middle A to D flat below the stave, at 'wo du die Gedanken hast' and, finally, a leap of a sixth downwards at the closing phrase, 'Wer hat dich *herbestellt*?' It all seems to suggest that Wolf saw, behind the girl's irate outburst, an aching heart longing for the faithless one to come back to her. True, the end of the postlude appears to indicate that her jealous rage flares up again, but this is merely to highlight the contradictory emotions by which the girl is moved.

The majority of the serious songs in the Italian volume are for men who pour out their heart in deep-felt passion for, or adoration of, the beloved. With very few exceptions, Wolf's women do not encompass the men's profound emotions and, instead, display jealous rage, scorn, mockery or, at best, a humorous tolerance and acceptance of their lovers' foibles. Yet, if they are shown in the grip of passionate love, it is sad, unhappy, tormented love that contrasts strongly with the rapture and serene contentment of their male counterparts.

It was to indicate the miniature form of most of his Italian songs that Wolf placed at the head of the published volume the tender, intimate 'Auch kleine Dinge können uns entzücken', a song that came chronologically as No. 16 in order of composition. The words, probably addressed to a petite mistress, are in praise of, to use a modern saying, 'small is beautiful'. The diminutive things – the pearl, the olive, the rose – are aptly symbolised by the broken semi-quaver chords and a stepwise descending melody in the left hand of the prelude which provides the material for the whole song. In the voice part, which is a paradigm of Wolf's subtle verbal treat-ment, there is a predominance of small intervals. It is a marvellously apt introduction to these songs.

It is psychologically interesting to observe that what kindled Wolf's imagination particularly strongly in the love poems is the image of a girl's facial features, especially her eyes and hair. As an illustration of this there are three songs of surpassing beauty, in the first two of which it is the eyes and, in the third, the hair that seem to have been Wolf's primary source of inspiration. In 'Der Mond hat eine schwere Klag'erhoben', the voice part tells, in beautifully inflected phrases, of the moon's complaint to the Lord that in counting his stars he found two missing – they are the mistress's eyes, whose light blinds the lover. Two-thirds of the song are almost throughout in the minor, but when the verses mention 'two of the most beautiful stars', the music turns suddenly to major in order to express the rapture by which the lover is seized. The halting movement of the moon's trajectory is suggested in the accompaniment by the rhythm (Ex. 17a). In 'Wenn du mich mit den Augen streifst', the extreme simplicity of the setting stands in inverse ratio to its beauty. It is pervaded by the rhythm (Ex. 17b):

Ex.17

This is a simple, ordinary pattern, but it seems to have had for Wolf a very special significance – perhaps the sublimation of erotic love; it recurs in at least five more songs, all in Part II (1896) of the Italian volume.[1] 'Und willst du deinen Liebsten sterben sehn', which compares the sweetheart's hair to a 'thread of pure gold', grows out of a little three-chord figure constantly repeated in changing intervals and harmonies (similar to 'Auf eine Christblume II') and appears in the second half of the song in diminished note-values, when it floats up to provide a shimmering, almost Debussian background for the muted voice part. Reconciliation of lovers is the theme of 'Nun lass uns Frieden schliessen' and 'Wir haben beide lange Zeit geschwiegen'. The first is a heart-easing song and full of declamatory felicities. Consider, for instance, the last couplet:

> Meinst du, dass, was so grossen Herrn gelingt,
> Ein Paar zufriedner Herzen nicht vollbringt?

The slight stress Wolf gives to 'Ein' by placing it on the first beat of the bar has the result of altering Heyse's 'a *pair*' to that of 'just *one* pair' of happy lovers, and so subtly reinforces the verbal meaning of the phrase. The second song, another superb piece, opens with a kind of introduction of four bars, which is never referred to again. The sad descending octaves suggest the lovers' estrangement, which

[1] 'Was für ein Lied', 'Wenn du, mein Geliebter, zum Himmel steigst', 'Was soll der Zorn', 'Benedeit die sel'ge Mutter', and 'Heut Nacht erhob ich mich'.

is followed by a truly magic figure at 'Die Engel, die herab vom Himmel fliegen' ('the angels flying down from heaven') which dominates the rest of the song.

Wolf at his most concentrated is seen in 'Heut Nacht erhob ich mich', in which an entire interior drama is enacted in not more than eighteen bars. It is infinitely intimate, almost hermetic music, of great harmonic interest and with an accompaniment that displays the string-quartet texture mentioned before. Similarly compressed is the immediately following 'Nicht länger kann ich singen' of fourteen bars – the material of which is parodistically expanded and varied in the woman's comic song 'Schweig einmal still', with which it forms a pair (see below).

Occasionally Wolf misreads the courtly conceit of a poem and, instead of seeing in it a game of love played according to the rules, takes it almost tragically. 'Wie viele Zeit verlor ich' is an instructive example of this. A lover complains about the time he lost in loving a girl, which forfeited him a place in Paradise. In Wolf's setting there is not the faintest hint of a smile; on the contrary, it expresses the utmost sadness, and the lover's pretended heartache and despair – the song is in G minor with some jarring dissonances (major ninths) – are eloquently summed up in the sad postlude. The beautiful 'Sterb'ich, so hüllt in Blumen' is in sentiment closely related to 'Bedeckt mich mit Blumen' in the *Spanish Song Book*, though musically its marked diatonic character strongly contrasts with the Spanish setting. Note the climax on F and E flat, the highest notes of the piece, at 'sterb'ich um *deinetwegen*'. The accompaniment is to be played *pianissimo* throughout.

Here and there Wolf interprets a line of the verse too literally. Take, for instance, 'Ihr seid die Allerschönste', in which Heyse renders the original 'Lo porti il vanto del Duomo di Siena' (literally: 'you have the advantage over the dome of Siena') into 'Der Dom von Siena muss sich vor dir neigen', meaning that the beloved far excels the cathedral of Siena in beauty. Wolf sets the metaphorical 'neigen' in a manner that clearly suggests that in his imagination he saw the cathedral actually *bowing* before the girl. But it is a touch of naivety which completely disappears in the music of the lover's limitless adoration of the girl. 'Gesegnet sei, durch den die Welt entstund' is impeccable, and one of the masterpieces in this volume. It provides an example of Wolf's art of distilling, even from mediocre verse, music which despite – or, perhaps, because of – its utter simplicity radiates an ineffable magic. The poem tells of God's all-embracing act of creation, and then passes from this general praise of his powers to a particular detail of it: the face of the beloved. A motive of falling wide intervals (octaves, sevenths and fifths) symbolises God's mighty act and pervades the whole setting. The climax is reached in the last line, with a crescendo up to 'He created', when suddenly the vocal phrase utters in hushed tones (*pp*) 'beauty and your face'. Note the sustained high F on '*An*gesicht'. The metaphors in 'Selig, ihr Blinden' cannot be called other than hyperbolic. The blind, the deaf, the dumb and the dead – all are blessed because they cannot experience the pangs of love any more. In contrast to the text, Wolf's setting shows admirable restraint. There is an interesting structural point about this song: instead of setting one line to one musical phrase, as was Wolf's wont, here he sets each of the four couplets to *one* phrase resulting in an appreciably broader sweep of the vocal line. Yet the accompaniment, with its relentless and inexorable crotchet movement, seems to belong to the world of the Spanish songs.

'Was für ein Lied' was the last song in order of composition but Wolf put it at the head of Part II of the published Italian volume. The question of the opening line, 'Where shall I find a song worthy of you?' is answered by the song itself, which is a paradigm of tenderness and adoration of the beloved; its main motive is the 'sublimation' figure (Ex. 17b) from 'Wenn du mich den Augen streifst'. The postlude restates the setting's main theme as though in response to the last line, 'a song that no man or woman, even the oldest, has ever heard until this day'. A love-song of almost religious devotion is the exquisite 'Und steht Ihr früh', in which the shape of the flowing quaver accompaniment is evocative of bells softly chiming in the distance – possibly in reference to the line, 'Then, when you go to holy Mass'. Wolf's mediant shifts (E major – A flat major – C major) here and in the following passage are significant. The poem of 'Schon streckt'ich aus' seems at first glance rather puzzling. A youth lies in bed, when he suddenly beholds a vision of his sweetheart. Up he jumps, dresses again and runs into the street with his lute and sings a serenade. But Wolf introduces perfect musical logic into his setting by allowing it to grow from a single figure whose ultimate shape dominates the lover's tender, muted serenade, which takes up the whole of the second half (Ex. 18 overleaf).

Ex.18

p (*dolce*)

The horn figure – (repeated several times) at once creates an out-of-doors atmosphere. The Italian verses of 'Benedeit die sel'ge Mutter' are neither a *rispetto* nor a *vilota*, but derive from a Venetian folksong in two stanzas. Heyse's rendering of the second stanza is an instructive instance of his tendency to over-intensify the original, as this comparison makes plain:

Ammirando la veghezza	Wenn ich aus der Ferne schmachte
Di bellezza così rara	Und betrachte deine Schöne,
Ti confesso, mia cara	Siehe wie ich beb'und stöhne,
Mi facesti sospirar;	Dass ich kaum es bergen kann!
E nel petto mi sentii	Und in meiner Brust gewaltsam
Una fiamma si vivace	Fühl'ich Flammen sich empören,
Che disturba la mia pace,	Die den Frieden mir zerstören,
Mi fa sempre delirar.	Ach, der Wahnsinn fass mich an!

Wolf added a literal repeat of the first stanza (thus obtaining the, for the mature composer, rarely employed A-B-A design) because he evidently felt he could not end on so disturbed an emotional note. But the discrepancy between the calm, diatonic first and third strophes and the feverishly excited chromatics of the second strophe is too great to make for a well-balanced song.

Men's songs in a lighter, humorous vein are comparatively rare in the Italian volume. To these belongs 'Hoffärtig seid Ihr, schönes Kind', which is an address to a belle whose haughty strutting is graphically caught in the proudly rising piano octaves of the accompaniment. The song is all scorn and contempt for the lady, except for a fleeting moment in bars 8/9, in which Wolf the psychologist reveals that the lover still has tender feelings for her. Note the marked slowing down of the *vivace* tempo (the female counterpart of this song is 'Du sagst mir') and the lyrical phrase ending on an expressive *appoggiatura* at 'Als kostet Euch zu viel ein holder *Gruss*' ('As if a kindly greeting would cost you too much effort'). Similar in idea is 'Lass sie nur gehn', in which a supposedly rejected lover pours out his venom on a girl as incorrigibly flirtatious as her twin sister in 'Ich hab'in Penna'. The song begins unpromisingly but gains in spirit and strength in the second half, in which the fickle creature is, curiously, compared with the river Arno, which has many tributaries (=admirers) in spring and none in summer. A setting entirely *sui generis* is the capital 'Geselle, woll'n wir uns in Kutten hüllen', set to a Venetian *vilota*, though the particular situation described might have stepped out of Boccaccio's *Decamerone*. A lecherous bogus monk wants to take 'confession' from a girl lying ill in bed. The sanctimonious whine and unctuousness with which he makes his proposal to the girl's mother, the latter's plea to come later, and the humbug's subsequent suggestion to shut door and window so as not to be disturbed in his 'holy' act – all this is limned in the music to uncanny effect. The main motive of the song would not be out of place in Strauss's *Till Eulenspiegel*:

Ex.19

'Geselle, woll'n wir uns in Kutten hüllen' is a test of a singer's easy management of different timbres in the service of characterisation. One of the few songs in the Italian volume that must be accounted an almost complete failure is 'O wüsstest du', in which the detachment of the music from the humour of the poem is so great that the two seem to run on two entirely different planes. The accompaniment is in the style of a three-part Bach 'invention', on which an indifferent voice part is superimposed.

About half the songs in the Italian volume are for women, and, as already intimated, there are only a few among them that can compare in profound serenity and depth of feeling with the best of the men's songs. We must, however, guard against ascribing this to Wolf's deliberate choice of poems; it is rather in the nature of the *rispetti* and *vilote* to show this bias. Such a deeply-felt female song is 'Mir ward gesagt', a poignant farewell to a departing lover. It opens in E minor and there are, in the accompaniment, stabbing clashes (seconds) on the first beat of virtually every other bar. In addition, Wolf introduces his 'separation' or 'isolation' motive – throbbing chords in the right hand and in the left a single line moving downwards (Ex. 20 overleaf).

These combine to create the feeling of a sad parting. But, as in 'Wer rief dich denn?', Wolf probes deeper into the girl's heart and discovers her secret hope that her lover will return to her from his distant journey and all will be well again: hence the revealing

changes of tempo and dynamics and, particularly, the modulation from a sorrowful E minor to a confident D major. Hardly less poignant, if more stylised, is 'Mein Liebster singt', in G minor, which is a simultaneous portrayal of two lovers: the youth (piano) in the dance-like serenade complete with guitar effect and a sarabande-like accentuation, in the bass, on the second beat of almost every bar; and the girl in the simple but expressive voice part, which speaks of her inconsolable sorrow – 'tears of blood' that have blinded her. (From the text one assumes that it is her mother who is the great obstacle to her joining the serenading youth.) Voice and piano move quite independently of each other, yet, as in all good counterpoint, the two fuse into a single musical event. This compressed double-portrait recalls Wolf's similar achievement in 'Das Ständchen' of the Eichendorff volume. In style, however, the song would seem to belong to the Spanish volume – note its dance character, and, in the piano part, the melismatic triplets in bar 10, the flourish in bar 11 and the augmented second in bar 25, all of which is faintly reminiscent of Spanish gypsy music. In 'Was soll der Zorn' it is the four opening words which seem to have determined the rhythmic shape of the vigorous main figure of the song. The poem tells of a girl who, seeing her lover in a rage, protests her innocence of any sin (evidently faithlessness), and urges him to pierce her heart with a dagger and so do away with her. There is, in this setting, high passion as well as a mortal threat verging on tragedy, as the postlude with its sinister upward thrust and the ending in C minor suggest.

There is a handful of women's songs expressing adoration and devotion almost in the same terms as the corresponding male songs. The first of these is 'Heb'auf dein blondes Haupt', a surpassingly beautiful setting in the vein of a lullaby in a gently flowing 12/8 time. A special feature here is the rising octave melody of the accompaniment, entering at the end of a vocal phrase or at a sustained note of it, by which Wolf achieves a wonderful natural continuation of the singing line.[1] With a single exception (bars 11 and 13) the dynamic level never rises above *piano*, and the emotional essence of the song is distilled into the most tender of postludes. In 'Wenn du, mein Liebster', an unhappy sweetheart has a vision of meeting her lover in heaven, when God will make 'one heart of our two loving hearts'. Her growing ecstasy is perfectly transmuted into terms of voice and piano, and the song reaches its climax, shortly before the end, in a passage the piano part of which is quasi-orchestral in character:

Ex.21

im Pa - ra - dies, um-glänzt von Him-mels flam - men.

f (in octaves)   *ff*

Wolf employs his 'sublimination' figure (Ex. 17b) to good effect, but the operatic upsurge of emotion in both voice and piano (with the postlude ending in a tremolo!) makes this setting less compelling than its finer male companion piece, 'Wenn du mich mit den Augen streifst'. Were it not for Schubert's exquisite 'Die grüne Farbe', we would, perhaps, hear 'Gesegnet sei das Grün' more frequently in the recital room than we do, for the song is pervaded by a warm, heart-easing serenity and contentment. Almost unique in Wolf, for its translucency and weightlessness, is 'O wär dein Haus durchsichtig'. The inspiration for the simple but striking accompaniment figure (Ex. 22 overleaf) evidently came to Wolf from the opening line of the verse, 'transparent as glass' (not from the patter of raindrops mentioned in the last line), which indeed evokes the flash and glitter of glass reflected in sunlight.

The melodic interest, as distinct from the motivic, resides entirely in the finely chiselled line of the voice part. Yet, as though by some alchemy, voice and piano fuse into one. Only 'Nixe Binsefuss' from

[1] In the Italian original the speaker is a woman; but in Heyse there is no indication of this, so that the song may also be sung by a man.

Ex.22

pp

the Mörike songs matches this song in its marvellous airiness.

Interestingly enough, Wolf reserves the large majority of his humorous or droll songs for women. There is, certainly, mocking laughter in the graceful 'Nein, junger Herr', with the three words generating the rhythmic patter of the main motive. But there is also a hint of unhappiness in this workaday mistress, who reproaches her lover that on holidays he looks for something better than her. The several *ritardandi* in this vivacious song (notably in the last line) are revealing, but the gay postlude covers up this undercurrent in the girl's feelings. Overt malice is the key-note of 'Du denkst mit einem Fädchen', Wolf seizing on this image for the thin thread of melody in the accompaniment's opening; and that the girl caught others with her charms is clearly indicated in chasing figures a little later. The *clou* of the song is the setting of the last line, illustrating her pretended swooning for love followed by her wicked laughter – 'I am in love, but not with you!'

Ex.23

ich bin ver liebt,_____ doch e - ben nicht in dich.

As with other humorous songs in the Italian volume, Wolf here sees the situation in the vivid terms of an operatic scene.

The Italian original of 'Wie lange schon' has a dry, mocking edge to it which is lost in Heyse's more sentimental rendering. Accordingly, Wolf opens in a wistful, if not indeed slightly *larmoyant*, vein, the voice part to be sung 'gefühlvoll' ('with feeling') above an accompaniment figure characterised by an augmented second, in a very slow tempo. The tempo redoubles (the original quavers of the motive now become semiquavers) at the appearance of a young lover, a violinist, who now plays 'diffidently and with hesitation' a chain of sighing *appoggiature*, closing his performance with a *slow* trill. All this is amusing but rather naive. Unlike the previous song, 'Mein Liebster ist so klein' is not a caricature but an affectionate description of an undersized lover, for which Wolf employs, strangely, an *appoggiatura* figure in the piano part, almost identical with that of Schubert's 'Geheimes'. The droll ending of this song has already been remarked upon. Perhaps it is the same lover who is the subject of 'Ihr jungen Leute', which is a brisk march song complete with drum taps and, at the end, a horn signal to underline the music's military atmosphere. A splendid song, and one illustrating a brightening of the mood without Wolf's having recourse to his mediant key-shifts, is 'Man sagt mir'. The girl's feelings grow from peevish defiance to warmth and affection and, finally, to passion for her lover, whose family does not approve of her. She first asks him to stay away from her, then to visit her secretly and more often and, eventually, to come *every* day, Wolf underlining the give-away *'alle Tage'* by sustaining a high E for nearly two full bars. In addition, the 'defiance' figure is, in a masterly way, so modified as to fit the girl's changing emotions perfectly. Entrancing in a different manner is 'Ein Ständchen euch zu bringen' (the last song of Part I of the Italian volume). It portrays an impetuous and swaggering young lover, who thinks of his sweetheart twenty-*five* hours out of twenty-four. The accompaniment, whose guitar character we have already mentioned, is similar to that of 'Heb'auf dein blondes Haupt', in that after every vocal phrase it gaily rises up with a scrap of crisp melody. 'Ich esse nun mein Brot' derives its chief effect from a juxtaposition of two strongly contrasted moods. In pathetic tones, accompanied by sorrowful *appoggiature*, a girl laments her fate of being loved by no one (E flat minor), but her despondent mood changes at once as she thinks of someone who might show her a little affection – perhaps a well-built man of her own age, truth to tell, a tiny old man of *fourteen* (E flat major). The second section is set to the music of a most engaging processional theme, suggesting that Wolf was imagining the girl to be marching about and looking right and left for the man of her desire. 'Mein Liebster hat mich zu Tische' is one of these songs the effect of which lies in the droll words rather than in their musical setting, except for the ending, in which the girl wickedly exaggerates the discomfort she suffered at a meal at the lover's: the table was small, the bread hard as stone and the knife blunt. Wolf conveys the hacking of the stale bread with the blunt knife with dramatic viciousness. In comparison, 'Du sagst mir, dass ich keine Fürstin sei' is more sophisticated. It is the counterpart to the male song, 'Hoffärtig seid Ihr' and is written in slightly varied strophic form, yet Wolf's apt projection at some verbal images is noteworthy, for example, the rumbling piano figure at 'und nicht in Staatskarossen' ('and not in a stagecoach') and the halting phrase at the lover riding on 'Schusters Rappen' ('Shanks's pony'). 'Ich liess mir sagen' is in invention not one of Wolf's vintage songs, but it shows his sense of irony almost as plainly as 'Bei einer Trauung' from the Mörike collection. Ever since handsome Toni has been feeling the pangs of love he has been starving himself by eating seven loaves at a sitting, and he subsequently fortifies himself with a large sausage and another seven loaves; unless Tonina eases his pain there will be famine and starvation in the land! Wolf opens and closes the song in the grave tones of a funeral march in C minor, and in between he enlivens the mock-seriousness by several climaxes; the last of which, at '*Hu*ngersnot' ('*fa*mine'), requires of the soprano a stentorian top A flat. In 'Wie soll ich fröhlich sein?', Wolf again goes behind the words and portrays an unhappy girl's contradictory emotions. On the surface she is up in arms against her lover who so sadly neglects her – he comes to her only about once in a hundred years, apparently because of some feud between the two families, but in her heart she feels only loving tenderness for him. The main motive, which follows the rhythm of the five opening words, dominates the accompaniment and invalidates her various statements of renunciation, as at bars 9 to 11 and 13 to 15, while its *fortissimo* version at the end clearly suggests that without her lover there can be no happiness for her. In the face of this and other settings containing similar psychological nuances, we can understand why Wolf considered the *Italian Song Book* as the most 'original of all my things'.

We have had occasion to refer to Wolf's pairing of songs by relating them to each other in idea as well as musical theme. Such a pair is 'Nicht länger kann ich singen' and 'Schweig'einmal still', which share a common key (A minor), time-signature (4/4) and, most importantly, the theme. How incompatible with each other the serenader of the first song and the girl of the second are, is seen in the parodistic distortion this theme now suffers. As if diminution of the original note-values and a faster tempo were not enough, Wolf adds vicious mordents, mocking grace-notes and trills, with suggestions of a donkey's braying into the bargain. This is dramatic irony at its most explicit. 'Verschling der Abgrund' is the song of a betrayed mistress who heaps the most terrible curses on her faithless lover. It is sheer melodrama, with almost interminable flourishes in the piano part and a predominantly high tessitura for the voice. Yet in an inspired performance, with a dramatic soprano capable of a ringing high A on 'Tod' ('death') and an able pianist, the song cannot fail to make an impact. An outstanding song among the women's humorous pieces is the immensely popular 'Ich hab'in Penna' with which Wolf concluded the published collection (in order of composition, it was the twentieth of the twenty-four settings of Part II of the Italian volume). For brilliance, rhythmic verve, and exuberance of mood this setting of a verse about an incorrigible flirt and her twenty-one lovers has no peer, except the 'Catalogue' aria of *Don Giovanni*. Wolf certainly remembered it when writing his song, witness such tell-tale evidence as, in the accompaniment, the rapid quaver movement and the whiplash scale passage at 'Maggione', while the voice part echoes Leporello's emphatic pauses on 'mâ in Ispâgna' in the girl's proud boast of having 'Zêhn in Castiglîone'. The breathtaking postlude is strongly reminiscent of the F major Study in Chopin's Op. 10. This sharp, glittering song is over in no time but then, as with most of the rest of the Italian volume, Wolf's motto appears to have been 'brevity is the soul of wit'.

The Last Published Songs (1897 and 1898)

Of the three late Reinick settings, 'Morgenstimmung' (1896) and 'Gesellenlied' (1888) claim special attention, though neither conforms to the canon of Wolf's really outstanding songs. It is interesting that initially the composer experienced great difficulties over the setting of the first poem, entitled by Reinick 'Morgenlied'. Wolf felt that the poem was not a 'Song' and not until he had rebaptised it 'Morning Mood' did his pen flow with ease. It seems that he considered the actual words of the poem as much less inspiring – it is indeed conventional – than the mood enshrined in them. (We noticed this before in the *Spanish* and *Italian Song Books*.) The song is indeed a mood-picture, reflecting the feelings aroused by the evocation of a rise from the darkness of night to a morning bathed in glorious sunlight, and closing on a climactic clarion call, 'Herr, lass uns kämpfen, lass uns siegen!' ('Lord, let us strive, let us conquer!'). The fervour with which Wolf imbued this phrase is seen from his setting of the word '*sie*gen' to a high G sharp sustained for over three and a half bars! (This is, incidentally, the same note on which the word 'Sieg' ('victory') is sung in the Mörike setting 'Der Genesene an die Hoffnung'.) That we should find Wolf's mediant shifts in the song is not surprising, seeing the significance this harmonic device possessed for him. The great success which 'Morgenstimmung' had at Wolf's last public appearance as accompanist of his songs (22 February 1897) pleased him immensely. 'Gesellenlied', composed in the year of his extraordinary creative flowering, is a most engaging song in varied strophic form. Its homely humour is open and direct, and it also touches a note of intimate tenderness in the third strophe which refers to the Master's young daughter. Wolf evidently identified the apprentice with the David of the *Meistersinger* and discreetly wove into the accompaniment the characteristic rhythm of the opening of the opera's overture. 'Skolie' (1889) is a rumbustious drinking-song with a bravura piano part but negligible as music pure and simple. So too is the Heine setting, 'Wo wird einst' (1888), and 'Lied des transferierten Zettel' (1889), Bottom's song from *A Midsummer Night's Dream*, in which the onomatopoeic illustration of a braying donkey is far less pointed than in the later 'Schweig einmal still' of the Italian volume. But there seems to be no rational explanation for the total neglect of the two Byron settings (1896), which bear the full stamp of Wolf's ripe maturity. 'Sonne der Schlummerlosen' is an apostrophe to the moon, the 'sun of the sleepless', turned by Wolf into a haunting nocturne in, significantly, C sharp minor. It is pervaded, in the bass of the accompaniment, by that syncopated rhythm suggestive of halting heartbeats which first appeared in the early Sturm song, 'Über Nacht' (1878), and pulses through the masterly 'Alle gingen, Herz, zur Ruh' from the Spanish collection. There is the icy air of a lunar landscape about this song, which in its last phrase 'hell, aber wie kalt!' ('clear, but, oh, how cold!') shows, as does a passage in 'Zur Ruh, zur Ruh!' (Ex. 6), the symbolic significance which Wolf associated with the opposition of high and low pitch – high E on 'hell' and C sharp below the stave on 'kalt'. The verses of 'Keine gleicht von allen Schönen' express a lover's deep romantic adoration of the beloved, to which Wolf responds with music of a highly wrought character, the vocal line of which displays a most remarkable pliability, even for Wolf.

There is a strong parallel between Brahms (his *bête noire*) and Wolf in their last song compositions. Brahms wrote towards the end of his life the *Vier ernste Gesänge*, while Wolf more or less terminated his creative activity with the three deeply serious Michelangelo settings (1897), the second of which expresses the same sentiments as the first of the Brahms songs.[1] Both cycles are for bass (or low baritone), a voice category best suited to their character. 'Naturally, the sculptor must sing bass,' said Wolf to Edmund Hellmer. Although Michelangelo's sonnets confronted Wolf with a new kind of poetry (in a translation by Walter Robert-Tornow), this did not lead to a new musical style (this is possibly connected with the outbreak of his mental illness some six months later) but to a reversion to the elaborate chromatic manner of some of the Mörike songs, such as 'Der Genesene an die Hoffnung' and 'Auf eine Christblume I'.

In 'Wohl denk'ich oft', Michelangelo reflects on the contrast between his past, when he was an obscure artist, and his present fame, when his name is known to all the world. This dichotomy is clearly mirrored in Wolf's setting. It begins in G minor in a withdrawn, introspective mood, which is followed by a section in the major, in which the words 'genannt in Lob und Tadel . . .' (my name is spoken whether in praise or dispraise . . .') are set to a beautifully arching vocal melody. The only blemishes on this fine song are the ensuing trumpet fanfares in a 'white' C major and the closing tremolo. The outstanding setting is undoubtedly 'Alles endet, was entstehet', which Wolf first thought of calling *Vanitas vanitarum*. Michelangelo confronts us with a terrifying vision of death and the corruption of flesh and, listening to Wolf's setting, sparse and skeletal in texture, we are reminded of what he said about 'bitter, inexorable truth – truth to the point of cruelty' being the supreme principle of his art. Significantly, C sharp minor is the key of the song, which is conceived with singular objectivity and with scarcely a note too many. In the opening two lines the muted vocal melody descends a tenth (from middle A to F sharp below the bass stave) and there is a stabbing clash between the E of the voice at '*Al*les' ('all') and the E sharp of the accompaniment, generated by what we nowadays call 'linear' counterpoint. Except for a momentary ray of light shed by the E major phrase, 'Menschen waren wir ja auch' ('We too were once alive'), the oppressively tenebrous mood never

[1] Wolf penned a fourth setting, 'Irdische und himmlische Liebe', but destroyed it because of his dissatisfaction with it.

changes. To say, however – as has been said – that the song is too terrible to be liked or loved is an aesthetic fallacy which confuses the play of the imagination on reality, which is the work of art, with reality. The last of the Michelangelo verses is a love-poem. Wolf's setting of 'Fühlt meine Seele' opens in E minor, in a mood of dark brooding, but as it unfolds the composer introduces his 'love' motive (Ex. 7) in the major; the depressive mood gradually begins to lift, and, finally, after intense chromatic writing, the music suddenly soars into the liberating diatonic climax, 'Darin sind, Herrin, deine Augen schuld' ('Guilty of this are your eyes, lady') – a last reminder of the inspirational power for Wolf of the image of a woman's eyes.

Wolf completed the Michelangelo settings in March 1897. Before the year was out, his mind sank slowly into growing night.

Index of Songs